stories
to
remember

LITERATURE TO ENJOY
STORIES TO ENJOY
POEMS TO ENJOY
PLAYS TO ENJOY
READINGS TO ENJOY

LITERATURE TO REMEMBER
STORIES TO REMEMBER
POEMS TO REMEMBER
PLAYS TO REMEMBER
READINGS TO REMEMBER

stories to remember

SOLOMON SCHLAKMAN

*Formerly Chairman of the English Department
Midwood High School, Brooklyn, New York
Instructor, School of Education
Brooklyn College, City University of New York*

MACMILLAN PUBLISHING COMPANY
NEW YORK

COLLIER MACMILLAN PUBLISHERS
LONDON

ACKNOWLEDGMENTS

For permission to use material in this book, grateful acknowledgment is made to the following:

Cooper Square Publishers, Inc.: For "Adjö Means Goodbye" by Carrie Allen Young from *Beyond the Angry Black* by John A. Williams. By permission of Cooper Square Publishers, Inc.

Doubleday & Company, Inc.: For "The Fun They Had," by Isaac Asimov. Reproduction in whole or part prohibited except by permission of N.E.A. Service, Inc. Copyright 1955 by Quinn Publishing Company, Inc. From *Earth Is Room Enough*, by Isaac Asimov. For "A Retrieved Reformation," from *Roads of Destiny*, by O. Henry. For "Enemy Territory" from *Dancers on the Shore* by William Melvin Kelley. Copyright © 1964 by William Melvin Kelley. Reprinted by permission of Doubleday and Company, Inc.

Barthold Fles: For "The New Kid," by Murray Heyert. First published in *Harper's Magazine*, June 1944.

Harcourt, Brace & World, Inc.: For "The Summer of the Beautiful White Horse," from *My Name Is Aram*, by William Saroyan. Copyright 1937, 1938, 1939, 1940 by William Saroyan. Reprinted by permission of Harcourt, Brace, & World, Inc.

Houghton Mifflin Company: For "Independence Day," from *The Big It*, by A. B. Guthrie, Jr. Copyright © 1960 by A. B. Guthrie, Jr. Reprinted by permission of the publisher, Houghton Mifflin Company. For "Jacob," from *The Plainsmen*, by Jack Schaefer. Copyright © 1963 by Houghton Mifflin Company. Reprinted by permission of the publisher, Houghton Mifflin Company.

Hutchinson & Co., Ltd.: For "Enemy Territory" from *Dancers on the Shore* by William Melvin Kelley. Reprinted by permission of Hutchinson & Co., Ltd.

Jonathan Cape, Ltd.: For "Death of a Tsotsi" by Alan Paton from *Debbie Go Home*. Reprinted by permission of Jonathan Cape, Ltd.

(acknowledgements continued on page 281)

Illustrations by John Gretzer and Douglas Jamieson

Macmillan Publishing Company
866 Third Avenue, New York, New York 10022
Collier Macmillan Canada, Inc.
Printed in the United States of America
ISBN 0-02-192430-9
6 7 8 9 10   93 92 91 90 89

CONTENTS

STORIES OF SUSPENSE

A RETRIEVED REFORMATION   *O. Henry*   2
LATHER AND NOTHING ELSE   *Hernando Téllez*   17

STORIES OF MOOD

HOP-FROG   *Edgar Allan Poe*   28
THE SUMMER OF THE BEAUTIFUL WHITE HORSE   45
   William Saroyan

STORIES OF THEME

THE BISHOP'S SILVER   *Victor Hugo*   60
WHAT MEN LIVE BY   *Leo Tolstoy*   85
DEATH OF A TSOTSI   *Alan Paton*   115

TWO STORIES OF THE WEST

MIDNIGHT   *Will James*   130
JACOB   *Jack Schaefer*   154

TWO STORIES ABOUT SPORTS

THICKER THAN WATER   *Paul Gallico*   178
INDEPENDENCE DAY   *A. B. Guthrie, Jr.*   190

STORIES ABOUT YOUNG PEOPLE

ENEMY TERRITORY   *William Melvin Kelley*   206
THE NEW KID   *Murray Heyert*   219
ADJO MEANS GOODBYE   *Carrie Allen Young*   239

STORIES OF THE FUTURE

THE ROCKET MAN   *Ray Bradbury*   252
THE FUN THEY HAD   *Isaac Asimov*   272

To the Reader

For thousands of years, people have enjoyed hearing stories and telling their own. Why are stories so popular? Because they take people from their own everyday world to a new and exciting world of adventure. Audiences share the characters' experiences and emotions.

Stories have also been popular because they help people cope with real life. The way characters handle their problems in an imaginary tale offers audiences a solution for handling their own problems in real life.

The stories in this book are meant to entertain you and help you understand real life. They are stories with adventure, humor, mystery, and excitement. But most of all, they are stories to remember.

STORIES
OF
SUSPENSE

A Retrieved Reformation

O. HENRY

Today, an expert safe-cracker is still called a
Jimmy Valentine, after the hero of this story. When
you have finished reading the story, you will
realize why Jimmy Valentine's burglarizing
activity has gone down into history.

A GUARD came to the prison shoe shop, where
Jimmy Valentine was assiduously stitching uppers, and es-
corted him to the front office. There the warden handed
Jimmy his pardon, which had been signed that morning by
the governor. Jimmy took it in a tired kind of way. He had
served nearly ten months of a four-year sentence. He had
expected to stay only about three months, at the longest.
When a man with as many friends on the outside as Jimmy
Valentine had is received in the "stir," it is hardly worth
while to cut his hair.

"Now, Valentine," said the warden, "you'll go out in the morning. Brace up, and make a man of yourself. You're not a bad fellow at heart. Stop cracking safes, and live straight."

"Me?" said Jimmy, in surprise. "Why, I never cracked a safe in my life."

"Oh, no," laughed the warden. "Of course not. Let's see, now. How was it you happened to get sent up on that Springfield job? Was it because you wouldn't prove an alibi for fear of compromising somebody in extremely high-toned society? Or was it simply a case of a mean old jury that had it in for you? It's always one or the other with you innocent victims."

"Me?" said Jimmy, still blankly virtuous. "Why, warden, I never was in Springfield in my life!"

"Take him back, Cronin," smiled the warden, "and fix him up with outgoing clothes. Unlock him at seven in the morning, and let him come to the bull-pen. Better think over my advice, Valentine."

At a quarter past seven on the next morning Jimmy stood in the warden's outer office. He had on a suit of the villainously fitting, ready-made clothes and a pair of the stiff, squeaky shoes that the state furnishes to its discharged compulsory guests.

The clerk handed him a railroad ticket and the five-dollar bill with which the law expects him to rehabilitate himself into good citizenship and prosperity. The warden gave him a cigar, and shook hands. Valentine, 9762, was chronicled on the books "Pardoned by Governor," and Mr. James Valentine walked out into the sunshine.

Disregarding the song of the birds, the waving green trees, and the smell of the flowers, Jimmy headed straight for a restaurant. There he tasted the first sweet joys of liberty in the shape of a broiled chicken and a bottle of white wine—followed by a cigar a grade better than the one the warden had given him. From there he proceeded leisurely to the depot. He tossed a quarter into the hat of a blind man sitting by the door, and boarded his train. Three hours set him down in a little town near the state line. He went to the café of one Mike Dolan and shook hands with Mike, who was alone behind the bar.

"Sorry we couldn't make it sooner, Jimmy, me boy," said Mike. "But we had the protest from Springfield to buck against, and the governor nearly balked. Feeling all right?"

"Fine," said Jimmy. "Got my key?"

He got his key and went upstairs, unlocking the door of a room at the rear. Everything was just as he had left it. There on the floor was still Ben Price's collar-button that had been torn from that eminent detective's shirt-band when they had overpowered Jimmy to arrest him.

Pulling out from the wall a folding bed, Jimmy slid back a panel in the wall and dragged out a dust-covered suitcase. He opened this and gazed fondly at the finest set of burglar's tools in the East. It was a complete set, made of specially tempered steel, the latest designs in drills, punches, braces and bits, jimmies, clamps, and augers, with two or three novelties, invented by Jimmy himself, in which he took pride. Over nine hundred dollars they had cost him to have made at ――――, a place where they made such things for the profession.

In half an hour Jimmy went downstairs and through the café. He was now dressed in tasteful and well-fitting clothes, and carried his dusted and cleaned suitcase in hand.

"Got anything on?" asked Mike Dolan genially.

"Me?" said Jimmy, in a puzzled tone. "I don't understand. I'm representing the New York Amalgamated Short Snap Biscuit Cracker and Frazzled Wheat Company."

This statement delighted Mike to such an extent that Jimmy had to take a seltzer-and-milk on the spot. He never touched "hard" drinks.

A week after the release of Valentine, 9762, there was a neat job of safe-burglary done in Richmond, Indiana, with no clue to the author. A scant eight hundred dollars was all that was secured. Two weeks after that a patented, improved, burglar-proof safe in Logansport was opened like a cheese to the tune of fifteen hundred dollars, currency; securities and silver untouched. That began to interest the rogue-catchers. Then an old-fashioned bank-safe in Jefferson City became active and threw out of its crater an eruption of bank notes amounting to five thousand dollars. The losses were now high enough to bring the matter up into Ben Price's class of work. By comparing notes, a remarkable similarity in the methods of the burglaries was noticed. Ben Price investigated the scenes of the robberies, and was heard to remark:

"That's Dandy Jim Valentine's autograph. He's resumed business. Look at that combination knob—jerked out as easy as pulling up a radish in wet weather. He's got the only clamps that can do it. And look how clean those tumblers were punched out! Jimmy never has to drill but one hole. Yes, I guess I want Mr. Valentine. He'll do his bit next time without any short-time or clemency foolishness."

Ben Price knew Jimmy's habits. He had learned them while working up the Springfield Case. Long jumps, quick getaways, no confederates, and a taste for good society— these ways had helped Mr. Valentine to become noted as

6   a successful dodger of retribution. It was given out that Ben Price had taken up the trail of the elusive cracksman, and other people with burglar-proof safes felt more at ease.

One afternoon Jimmy Valentine and his suitcase climbed out of the mail-hack in Elmore, a little town five miles off the railroad down in the black-jack country of Arkansas. Jimmy, looking like an athletic young senior just home from college, went down the board sidewalk toward the hotel.

A young lady crossed the street, passed him at the corner, and entered a door over which was the sign "The Elmore Bank." Jimmy Valentine looked into her eyes, forgot what he was, and became another man. She lowered her eyes and colored slightly. Young men of Jimmy's style and looks were scarce in Elmore.

Jimmy collared a boy that was loafing on the steps of the bank as if he were one of the stockholders, and began to ask him questions about the town, feeding him dimes at intervals. By and by the young lady came out, looking royally unconscious of the young man with the suitcase, and went her way.

'Isn't that young lady Miss Polly Simpson?" asked Jimmy.

"Naw," said the boy. "She's Annabel Adams. Her pa owns this bank. What'd you come to Elmore for? Is that a gold watch-chain? I'm going to get a bulldog. Got any more dimes?"

Jimmy went to the Planter's Hotel, registered as Ralph D. Spencer, and engaged a room. He leaned on the desk and declared his platform to the clerk. He said he had come to Elmore to look for a location to go into business. How was the shoe business, now, in the town? He had thought of the shoe business. Was there an opening?

The clerk was impressed by the clothes and manner of Jimmy. He, himself, was something of a pattern of fashion to the thinly gilded youth of Elmore, but he now perceived his shortcomings. While trying to figure out Jimmy's manner of tying his four-in-hand he cordially gave information.

Yes, there ought to be a good opening in the shoe line. There wasn't an exclusive shoe-store in the place. The dry-goods and the general stores handled them. Business in all lines was fairly good. Hoped Mr. Spencer would decide to locate in Elmore. He would find it a pleasant town to live in, and the people very sociable.

Mr. Spencer thought he would stop over in the town a few days and look over the situation. No, the clerk needn't call the boy. He would carry up his suitcase himself; it was rather heavy.

Mr. Ralph Spencer, the phoenix that arose from Jimmy Valentine's ashes—ashes left by the flame of a sudden and transforming attack of love—remained in Elmore, and prospered. He opened a shoe-store and secured a good run of trade.

Socially he was also a success and made many friends. And he accomplished the wish of his heart. He met Miss Annabel Adams, and became more and more captivated by her charms.

At the end of a year the situation of Mr. Ralph Spencer was this: he had won the respect of the community, his shoe-store was flourishing, and he and Annabel were engaged to be married in two weeks. Mr. Adams, the typical, plodding country banker, approved of Spencer. Annabel's pride in him almost equaled her affection. He was as much at home in the family of Mr. Adams and that of Annabel's married sister as if he were already a member.

8   One day Jimmy sat down in his room and wrote this letter, which he mailed to the safe address of one of his old friends in St. Louis:

Dear Old Pal:

I want you to be at Sullivan's place in Little Rock, next Wednesday night, at nine o'clock. I want you to wind up some little matters for me. And, also, I want to make you a present of my kit of tools. I know you'll be glad to get them —you couldn't duplicate the lot for a thousand dollars. Say, Billy, I've quit the old business—a year ago. I've got a nice store. I'm making an honest living, and I'm going to marry the finest girl on earth two weeks from now. It's the only life, Billy—the straight one. I wouldn't touch a dollar of another man's money now for a million. After I get married I'm going to sell out and go West, where there won't be so much danger of having old scores brought up against me. I tell you, Billy, she's an angel. She believes in me; and I wouldn't do another crooked thing for the whole world. Be sure to be at Sully's, for I must see you. I'll bring along the tools with me.

Your old friend,
Jimmy

On the Monday night after Jimmy wrote this letter, Ben Price jogged unobtrusively into Elmore in a livery buggy. He lounged about town in his quiet way until he found out what he wanted to know. From the drug-store across the street from Spencer's shoe-store, he got a good look at Ralph D. Spencer.

"Going to marry the banker's daughter are you, Jimmy?" said Ben to himself, softly. "Well, I don't know!"

The next morning, Jimmy took breakfast at the Adamses. He was going to Little Rock that day to order his wedding-suit and buy something nice for Annabel. That would be the first time he had left town since he came to Elmore. It had been more than a year now since those last professional "jobs," and he thought he could safely venture out.

After breakfast quite a family party went downtown together—Mr. Adams, Annabel, Jimmy, and Annabel's married sister with her two little girls, aged five and nine. They came by the hotel where Jimmy still boarded and he ran up to his room and brought along his suitcase. Then they went on to the bank. There stood Jimmy's horse and buggy and Dolph Gibson, who was going to drive him over to the railroad station.

All went inside the high, carved oak railings into the banking room—Jimmy included, for Mr. Adams' future son-in-law was welcome anywhere. The clerks were pleased to be greeted by the good-looking, agreeable young man who was going to marry Miss Annabel. Jimmy set his suitcase down. Annabel, whose heart was bubbling with happiness and lively youth, put on Jimmy's hat, and picked up the suitcase. "Wouldn't I make a nice drummer?" said Annabel. "My, Ralph, how heavy it is! Feels like it was full of gold bricks."

"Lot of nickel-plated shoe-horns in there," said Jimmy coolly, "that I'm going to return. Thought I'd save express charges by taking them up. I'm getting awfully economical."

The Elmore Bank had just put in a new safe and vault. Mr. Adams was very proud of it, and insisted on an inspection by everyone. The vault was a small one, but it had a new, patented door. It fastened with three solid steel bolts thrown simultaneously with a single handle, and had a time-

10　lock. Mr. Adams beamingly explained its workings to Mr. Spencer, who showed a courteous but not too intelligent interest. The two children, May and Agatha, were delighted by the shining metal and funny clock and knobs.

While they were thus engaged Ben Price sauntered in and leaned on his elbow, looking casually inside between the railings. He told the teller that he didn't want anything; he was just waiting for a man he knew.

Suddenly there was a scream or two from the women, and a commotion. Unperceived by the elders, May, the nine-year-old girl, in a spirit of play, had shut Agatha in the vault. She had then shot the bolts and turned the knob of the combination as she had seen Mr. Adams do.

The old banker sprang to the handle and tugged at it for a moment. "The door can't be opened," he groaned. "The clock hasn't been wound nor the combination set."

Agatha's mother screamed again, hysterically.

"Hush!" said Mr. Adams, raising his trembling hand. "All be quiet for a moment. Agatha," he called as loudly as he could. "Listen to me." During the following silence they could just hear the faint sound of the child wildly shrieking in the dark vault in a panic of terror.

"My precious darling!" wailed the mother. "She will die of fright! Open the door! Oh, break it open! Can't you men do something?"

"There isn't a man nearer than Little Rock who can open that door," said Mr. Adams, in a shaky voice. "My God! Spencer, what shall we do? That child—she can't stand it long in there. There isn't enough air, and, besides, she'll go into convulsions from fright."

Agatha's mother, frantic now, beat the door of the vault with her hands. Somebody wildly suggested dynamite. Annabel turned to Jimmy, her large eyes full of anguish, but not yet despairing. To a woman nothing seems quite impossible to the powers of the man she worships.

"Can't you do something, Ralph—try, won't you?"

He looked at her with a queer, soft smile on his lips and in his keen eyes.

"Annabel," he said, "give me that rose you are wearing, will you?"

Hardly believing that she heard him aright, she unpinned the bud from the bosom of her dress, and placed it in his hand. Jimmy stuffed it into his vest-pocket, threw off his coat, and pulled up his shirt-sleeves. With that act Ralph D. Spencer passed away and Jimmy Valentine took his place.

"Get away from the door, all of you," he commanded shortly.

He set his suitcase on the table, and opened it flat. From that time on he seemed to be unconscious of the presence of anyone else. He laid out the shining, queer implements swiftly and orderly, whistling softly to himself as he always did when at work. In a deep silence and immovable, the others watched him as if under a spell.

Jimmy's pet drill was biting smoothly into the steel door. In ten minutes—breaking his own burglarious record—he threw back the bolts and opened the door.

Agatha, almost collapsed, but safe, was gathered into her mother's arms.

Jimmy Valentine put on his coat and walked outside the railings toward the front door. As he went he thought he heard a far-away voice that he once knew call "Ralph!" But he never hesitated.

At the door a big man stood somewhat in his way.

"Hello, Ben!" said Jimmy, still with his strange smile. "Got around at last, have you? Well, let's go. I don't know that it makes much difference, now."

12   And then Ben Price acted rather strangely.

"Guess you're mistaken, Mr. Spencer," he said. "Don't believe I recognize you. Your buggy's waiting for you, ain't it?"

And Ben Price turned and strolled down the street.

About the Author

O. Henry (whose real name was William Sydney Porter) was born in Greensboro, North Carolina, in 1862. At the age of fifteen he left school to go to work, finding his way to Texas where he became in turn a bank teller and a newspaper man. Accused later of stealing funds from his bank, William Porter fled Texas in the company of several men of rather bad reputation, whom he was to use later as characters in his stories. He returned to Texas in 1897 to serve a term in the penitentiary. It was in prison that he began writing stories under the pen name of O. Henry. On his release, he went to New York City. There he was fond of roaming the streets and talking to all kinds of characters. Most of his stories were written in New York, where he died at the age of forty-eight.

It was O. Henry who made the surprise ending a popular story-telling device. He got the idea for "A Retrieved Reformation" from a prison pal. The story was so popular when it was published that it became a Broadway play entitled *Alias Jimmy Valentine,* a motion picture of the same name, and the basis of a popular song entitled "Jimmy Valentine."

FOR DISCUSSION

Understanding the Story

1. When we sit down to read a typical suspense story, we generally do so only for pleasure; we rarely look for deep ideas or serious discussions of serious problems.

   "A Retrieved Reformation" is such a story, a kind of crime suspense story. To enjoy it, the reader must forget or ignore some of his usual serious ideas about crime and criminals.

   Which of our usual ideas have to be put aside in reading this story? Why?

2. In most suspense stories, an author must do two things: first, he must make the reader *care* about the hero of the story; second, he must arrange the story so that the hero is involved in some kind of conflict which gets constantly more exciting or dangerous, so that the reader wants to read on and on.

   Even before Jimmy reformed, the chances are that you were "on his side," that you cared about him. How did the author get you to like Jimmy, even though he was a criminal? Reviewing these parts of the story will help you to think through to a good answer:
   a. the conversation with the warden
   b. Jimmy's deeds the first day out of jail
   c. his conversation with Mike Dolan
   d. his activities, his techniques, his behavior in the next few weeks

3. a. Jimmy has two conflicts to face in this story. One of them runs through the whole story, but he is not even aware of it; only the reader knows. With whom does he have this conflict?
   b. Look back at the story and observe at *what points* O. Henry reminded us of this conflict. Can you see how the author arranged it so that, as Jimmy became more and more successful, the reader became more and more worried?

    c. The other important conflict is not really described in the story, but the reader knows it must have taken place—a conflict *in Jimmy's mind* that day in the bank. What do you suppose this conflict was? How had the author prepared us for Jimmy's decision?

4. What do you suppose happened after the close of the story?

VOCABULARY GROWTH

Using Context to Unlock Word Meanings

In most stories that you read, you will encounter some unfamiliar words. What have you done about them in the past? Have you just skipped and ignored them?

If so, you have probably missed a great deal. True, not every new word you meet in a story is important. But many probably are. Such words often are key words in the understanding of a character, or of some important incident.

1. Sometimes the manner in which a new word is used in a sentence gives you some idea of its meaning, making the use of a dictionary unnecessary. For example, one of O. Henry's sentences reads:

    "The clerk handed him a railroad ticket and the five-dollar bill with which the law expects him to *rehabilitate* himself into good citizenship and prosperity."

The fact that Jimmy is getting a train ticket and money on release from jail and the mention of good citizenship and prosperity at the close of the sentence—these details should help you to guess what *rehabilitate* must mean. What guess would you make? Check your guess with the dictionary.

The surroundings of a word that help you to get its meaning are called the *context* of the word.

2. Sometimes the context is not of much help. A wise thing to do then is to use the dictionary.

The first sentence of the story tells you something important about Jimmy's character, but you miss the point entirely if you don't know what *assiduously* means. The context in this case is not helpful:

> "A guard came to the prison shoe shop, where Jimmy Valentine was *assiduously* stitching uppers. . . ."

In this case, you should look up the meaning of the unfamiliar word. The fact that Jimmy was *assiduous* even in the prison shoe shop tells us something important about his character.

3. Which of the italicized words in the sentences below can you understand from the context? Which do you need to look up? All of the words convey important ideas in the story. Be sure you can explain both the italicized word and the important idea it conveys.

a. "How was it you happened to get sent up on that Springfield job? Was it because you wouldn't prove an alibi for fear of *compromising* somebody in extremely high-toned society?"

b. " 'Yes, I guess I want Mr. Valentine. He'll do his bit next time without any short-time or *clemency* foolishness.' "

c. "Long jumps, quick getaways, no confederates, and a taste for good society—these ways helped Mr. Valentine to become noted as a successful dodger of *retribution*."

d. "It was given out that Ben Price had taken up the trail of the *elusive* cracksman. . . ."

e. "Mr. Ralph Spencer, the *phoenix* that arose from Jimmy Valentine's ashes—. . . remained in Elmore, and prospered."

f. "On the Monday night after Jimmy wrote this letter, Ben Price jogged *unobtrusively* into Elmore in a livery buggy."

g. "Agatha's mother, *frantic* now, beat the door of the vault with her hands."

h. "He laid out the shining, queer *implements* swiftly and orderly. . . ."

FOR COMPOSITION

1. The events of the last part of this story took place in the morning. Write a continuation of the story, telling what you imagine must have taken place later that day.

2. Ben Price will have to go back to police headquarters in your home town without the man he was supposed to get.

   What explanation do you suppose he will offer to his superior officer? Write an account of Ben's return to headquarters and the story he might tell when he gets there.

Lather
and
Nothing Else

HERNANDO TÉLLEZ

Your enemy, a vile killer, is sitting in the
barber's chair and you are standing over him,
your razor in your hand, ready to "shave" him.
What are you thinking?

HE CAME in without a word. I was stropping my
best razor. And when I recognized him I started to shake.
But he did not notice. To cover my nervousness, I went on
honing the razor. I tried the edge with the tip of my thumb
and took another look at it against the light.

Meanwhile, he was taking off his cartridge-studded belt
with the pistol holster suspended from it. He put it on a
hook in the wardrobe and hung his cap above it. Then he
turned full around toward me and, loosening his tie, remarked: "It's hot as the devil. I want a shave." With that
he took his seat.

17

I estimated he had a four days' growth of beard. The four days he had been gone on the last foray after our men. His face looked burnt, tanned by the sun.

I started to work carefully on the shaving soap. I scraped some slices from the cake, dropped them into the mug, then added a little lukewarm water, and stirred with the brush. The lather soon began to rise.

"The fellows in the troop must have just about as much beard as I." I went on stirring up lather.

"But we did very well, you know. We caught the leaders. Some of them we brought back dead, others are still alive. But they'll all be dead soon."

"How many did you take?" I asked.

"Fourteen. We had to go pretty far in to find them. But now they're paying for it. And not one will escape; not a single one."

He leaned back in the chair when he saw the brush in my hand, full of lather. I had not yet put the sheet on him. I was certainly flustered. Taking a sheet from the drawer, I tied it around my customer's neck.

He went on talking. He evidently took it for granted I was on the side of the existing regime.

"The people must have gotten a scare with what happened the other day," he said.

"Yes," I replied, as I finished tying the knot against his nape, which smelt of sweat.

"Good show, wasn't it?"

"Very good," I answered, turning my attention now to the brush. The man closed his eyes wearily and awaited the cool caress of the lather.

I had never had him so close before. The day he ordered the people to file through the schoolyard to look upon the four rebels hanging there, my path had crossed his briefly.

But the sight of those mutilated bodies kept me from paying   19
attention to the face of the man who had been directing
it all and whom I now had in my hands.

It was not a disagreeable face, certainly. And the beard,
which aged him a bit, was not unbecoming. His name was
Torres. Captain Torres.

I started to lay on the first coat of lather. He kept his
eyes closed.

"I would love to catch a nap," he said, "but there's a lot
to be done this evening."

I lifted the brush and asked, with pretended indifference:
"A firing party?"

"Something of the sort," he replied, "but slower."

"All of them?"

"No, just a few."

I went on lathering his face. My hands began to tremble
again. The man could not be aware of this, which was lucky
for me. But I wished he had not come in. Probably many of
our men had seen him enter the shop. And with the enemy
in my house I felt a certain responsibility.

I would have to shave his beard just like any other, carefully, neatly, just as though he were a good customer, taking
heed that not a single pore should emit a drop of blood.
Seeing to it that the blade did not slip in the small whorls.
Taking care that the skin was left clean, soft, shining, so
that when I passed the back of my hand over it not a single
hair should be felt. Yes. I was secretly a revolutionary, but
at the same time I was a conscientious barber, proud of the
way I did my job. And that four-day beard presented a
challenge.

I took up the razor, opened the handle wide, releasing
the blade, and started to work, downward from one sideburn. The blade responded to perfection. The hair was

20   tough and hard; not very long, but thick. Little by little the skin began to show through. The razor gave out its usual sound as it gathered up layers of soap mixed with bits of hair. I paused to wipe it clean, and taking up the strop once more went about improving its edge, for I am a painstaking barber.

The man, who had kept his eyes closed, now opened them, put a hand out from under the sheet, felt of the part of his face that was emerging from the lather, and said to me: "Come at six o'clock this evening to the school."

"Will it be like the other day?" I asked, stiff with horror.

"It may be even better," he replied.

"What are you planning to do?"

"I'm not sure yet. But we'll have a good time."

Once more he leaned back and shut his eyes. I came closer, the razor on high.

"Are you going to punish all of them?" I timidly ventured.

"Yes, all of them."

The lather was drying on his face. I must hurry. Through the mirror, I took a look at the street. It appeared about as usual: there was the grocery shop with two or three customers. Then I glanced at the clock: two-thirty.

The razor kept descending. Now from the other sideburn downward. It was a blue beard, a thick one. He should let it grow like some poets, or some priests. It would suit him well. Many people would not recognize him. And that would be a good thing for him, I thought, as I went gently over all the throat line. At this point you really had to handle your blade skillfully, because the hair, while scantier, tended to fall into small whorls. It was a curly beard. The pores might open, minutely, in this area and let out a tiny drop of blood. A good barber like myself stakes his reputation on not permitting that to happen to any of his customers.

And this was indeed a special customer. How many of ours had he sent to their death? How many had he mutilated? It was best not to think about it. Torres did not know I was his enemy. Neither he nor the others knew it. It was a secret shared by very few, just because that made it possible for me to inform the revolutionaries about Torres' activities in the town and what he planned to do every time he went on one of his raids to hunt down rebels. So it was going to be very difficult to explain how it was that I had him in my hands and then let him go in peace, alive, clean-shaven.

His beard had now almost entirely disappeared. He looked younger, several years younger than when he had come in. I suppose that always happens to men who enter and leave barbershops. Under the strokes of my razor Torres was rejuvenated; yes, because I am a good barber, the best in this town, and I say this in all modesty.

A little more lather here under the chin, on the Adam's apple, right near the great vein. How hot it is! Torres must be sweating just as I am. But he is not afraid. He is a tranquil man, who is not even giving thought to what he will do to his prisoners this evening. I, on the other hand, polishing his skin with this razor but avoiding the drawing of blood, careful with every stroke—I cannot keep my thoughts in order.

Confound the hour he entered my shop! I am a revolutionary but not a murderer. And it would be so easy to kill him. He deserves it. Or does he? No, damn it! No one deserves the sacrifice others make in becoming assassins. What is to be gained by it? Nothing. Others and still others

22   keep coming, and the first kill the second, and then these kill the next, and so on until everything becomes a sea of blood. I could cut his throat, so, swish, swish! He would not even have time to moan, and with his eyes shut he would not even see the shine of the razor or the gleam in my eye.

But I'm shaking like a regular murderer. From his throat a stream of blood would flow on the sheet, over the chair, down on my hands, onto the floor. I would have to close the door. But the blood would go flowing, along the floor, warm, indelible, not to be stanched, until it reached the street, like a small scarlet river.

I'm sure that with a good strong blow, a deep cut, he would feel no pain. He would not suffer at all. And what would I do then with the body? Where would I hide it? I would have to flee, leave all this behind, take shelter far away, very far away. But they would follow until they caught up with me. "The murderer of Captain Torres. He slit his throat while he was shaving him. What a cowardly thing to do!"

And others would say: "The avenger of our people. A name to remember"—my name here. "He was the town barber. No one knew he was fighting for our cause."

And so, which will it be? Murderer or hero? My fate hangs on the edge of this razor blade. I can turn my wrist slightly, put a bit more pressure on the blade, let it sink in. The skin will yield like silk, like rubber, like the strop. There is nothing more tender than a man's skin, and the blood is always there, ready to burst forth. A razor like this cannot fail. It is the best one I have.

But I don't want to be a murderer. No, sir. You came in to be shaved. And I do my work honorably. I don't want to stain my hands with blood. Just with lather, and nothing else. You are an executioner; I am only a barber. Each one to his job. That's it. Each one to his job.

The chin was now clean, polished, soft. The man got up and looked at himself in the glass. He ran his hand over the skin and felt its freshness, its newness.

"Thanks," he said. He walked to the wardrobe for his belt, his pistol, and his cap. I must have been very pale, and I felt my shirt soaked with sweat. Torres finished adjusting his belt buckle, straightened his gun in its holster, and, smoothing his hair mechanically, put on his cap. From his trousers pocket he took some coins to pay for the shave. And he started toward the door. On the threshold he stopped for a moment, and turning toward me he said:

"They told me you would kill me. I came to find out if it was true. But it's not easy to kill. I know what I'm talking about."

About the Author

Hernando Téllez, a South American writer and diplomat, comes from a continent where revolutions occur frequently. He was born in Bogotá, Colombia, in 1908, and began his professional life as a journalist. Later, he served as a city official in Bogotá, as a consular representative in France, and as a national senator in 1943–1944. More recently he has been Colombia's ambassador to the United Nations Educational Scientific and Cultural Organization. Mr. Téllez has maintained his interest in journalism and writing and has published many essays and stories in Spanish.

FOR DISCUSSION

Understanding the Story

1. Although we are *told* very little about the setting of this story (where it takes place, when it takes place, under what conditions), except that the scene is a barber shop, a good deal is hinted by the author. What evidence does the story offer in answer to these questions?

   a. Where is the country of Torres and the barber?

   b. What kind of government exists there?

   c. Why are there so many executions?

2. What were *your* feelings about Captain Torres, sitting in that barber's chair? What details made you feel as you did?

3. The barber says, "I am a revolutionary, but not a murderer." How does the barber differ from the type of revolutionary that most people picture in their minds?

4. What made the barber finally act as he did? A key sentence to consider in answering this question is the barber's statement on page 21: "No one deserves the sacrifice others make in becoming assassins." (Who are the "others"?)

5. How do you explain the strange statement Torres makes as he leaves the barber shop?

6. What is your final opinion of the barber? Is he a coward at heart? Do you respect him?

The Art of Creating Suspense

1. Some stories create suspense immediately; others build it up very gradually. Which type is this story? Support your answer.

2. To create suspense, you have learned, a writer must make the reader sympathize with and *care about* the hero. How did the writer make you care about the barber in this story?

3. You have also learned that suspense depends on a conflict or a series of conflicts in which the excitement keeps increasing. This conflict is most often between people—between the hero (or heroine) and others; sometimes, however, the conflict may be *within the mind* of a person. In the latter case, we call the suspense *psychological*.

   a. Does the suspense in this story depend mostly upon the conflict between the barber and Torres, or upon the conflict in the mind of the barber? Explain.

   b. In this story, a barber shaves a customer, and the barber *thinks* as he shaves. Both the shaving process and the thinking are described in detail. Review the story; see if you can trace how the barber's particular thoughts at certain *particular stages* in the shave help to build up increasing suspense.

VOCABULARY GROWTH

Using Context to Unlock Word Meanings

Although the vocabulary of this story is generally simple, there are a few words which you may not be familiar with, which are nevertheless helpful in understanding completely the feelings of the barber. In most cases, the context—the surroundings of the words—will enable you to guess the meaning; in one or two cases you may need a dictionary.

1. Early in the story, for example, you read that Torres has been gone for days on "a *foray* after our men." The phrase in quotation marks helps you to realize immediately why the barber is so nervous about his customer, and the context provides a clear clue to the meaning of *foray*. What guess would you make as to the meaning of the word?

2. Using either context clues or your dictionary, indicate the meaning of each italicized word in the sentences that follow:

   a. "He [Torres] went on talking. He evidently took it for granted I was on the side of the existing *regime*."

b. "The day he ordered the people ... to look upon the four rebels hanging there, my path had crossed his briefly. But the sight of those *mutilated* bodies kept me from paying attention to the face of the man ... whom I now had in my hands."

c. " 'I would love to catch a nap,' he said, 'but there's a lot to be done this evening.' "
"I lifted the brush and asked, with pretended *indifference:* 'A firing party?' "

d. "He looked younger.... Under the strokes of my razor, Torres was *rejuvenated....*" (*Re,* as a prefix, means "again" or "back"; what does *juvenile* mean?)

e. "But the blood would go flowing, along the floor, warm, indelible, not to be *stanched,* until it reached the street, like a small scarlet river."

FOR COMPOSITION

1. Was the barber right or wrong in not killing Torres? Defend your answer in a short composition.

2. Try retelling this story as Torres would tell it. See if you can build up suspense by describing the shave and your thoughts, as you sit in the chair and the razor goes up and down.

3. Sitting in a barber's chair is not always so serious as it is in this story. Write a humorous composition, describing your thoughts or your feelings as you sit in the barber shop (or beauty parlor).

STORIES
OF
MOOD

Hop-Frog

EDGAR ALLAN POE

Horror in real life is—horror! But in a well-told
story, horror can be enjoyable. Here is a story by
the master of all stories of terror.

I NEVER knew any one so keenly alive to a joke as
the king was. He seemed to live only for joking. To tell a
good story of the joke kind, and to tell it well, was the surest
road to his favor. Thus it happened that his seven ministers
were all noted for their accomplishments as jokers. They all
took after the king, too, in being large, corpulent, oily men,
as well as inimitable jokers. Whether people grow fat by
joking, or whether there is something in fat itself which
predisposes to a joke, I have never been quite able to deter-
mine; but certain it is that a lean joker is a *rara avis in terris*.

About the refinements, or, as he called them, the "ghosts"
of wit, the king troubled himself very little. He had an especial admiration for *breadth* in a jest, and would often put up
with *length*, for the sake of it. Overniceties wearied him ...
upon the whole, practical jokes suited his taste far better
than verbal ones.

At the date of my narrative, professional jesters had not
altogether gone out of fashion at court. Several of the great

28

continental "powers" still retained their "fools," who wore motley, with caps and bells, and who were expected to be always ready with sharp witticisms, at a moment's notice, in consideration of the crumbs that fell from the royal table.

Our king, as a matter of course, retained his "fool." The fact is, he *required* something in the way of folly—if only to counterbalance the heavy wisdom of the seven wise men who were his ministers—not to mention himself.

His fool, or professional jester, was not *only* a fool, however. His value was trebled in the eyes of the king, by the fact of his being also a dwarf and a cripple. Dwarfs were as common at court, in those days, as fools; and many monarchs would have found it difficult to get through their days (days are rather longer at court than elsewhere) without both a jester to laugh *with*, and a dwarf to laugh *at*. But, as I have already observed, your jesters, in ninety-nine cases out of a hundred, are fat, round, and unwieldy—so that it was no small source of self-gratulation with our king that, in Hop-Frog (this was the fool's name), he possessed a triplicate treasure in one person.

I believe the name "Hop-Frog" was *not* that given to the dwarf by his sponsors at baptism, but it was conferred upon him, by general consent of the seven ministers, on account of his inability to walk as other men do. In fact, Hop-Frog could only get along by a sort of interjectional gait—something between a leap and a wriggle,—a movement that afforded illimitable amusement, and of course consolation, to the king, for (notwithstanding the protuberance of his stomach and a constitutional swelling of the head) the king, by his whole court, was accounted a capital figure.

But although Hop-Frog, through the distortion of his legs, could move only with great pain and difficulty along a road

30   or floor, the prodigious muscular power which nature seemed
to have bestowed upon his arms, by way of compensation for
deficiency in the lower limbs, enabled him to perform many
feats of wonderful dexterity, where trees or ropes were in
question, or anything else to climb. At such exercises he certainly much more resembled a squirrel, or a small monkey,
than a frog.

I am not able to say, with precision, from what country
Hop-Frog originally came. It was from some barbarous
region, however, that no person ever heard of—a vast
distance from the court of our king. Hop-Frog, and a young
girl very little less dwarfish than himself (although of exquisite proportions, and a marvelous dancer), had been
forcibly carried off from their respective homes in adjoining
provinces, and sent as presents to the king, by one of his
ever-victorious generals.

Under these circumstances, it is not to be wondered at
that a close intimacy arose between the two little captives.
Indeed, they soon became sworn friends. Hop-Frog, who,
although he made a great deal of sport, was by no means
popular, had it not in his power to render Trippetta many
services; but *she,* on account of her grace and exquisite
beauty (although a dwarf), was universally admired and
petted; so she possessed much influence; and never failed
to use it, whenever she could, for the benefit of Hop-Frog.

On some grand state occasion—I forget what—the king
determined to have a masquerade; and whenever a masquerade, or any thing of that kind, occurred at our court,
then the talents both of Hop-Frog and Trippetta were sure
to be called into play. Hop-Frog, in especial, was so inventive
in the way of getting up pageants, suggesting novel characters, and arranging costumes for masked balls, that nothing
could be done, it seems, without his assistance.

The night appointed for the *fête* had arrived. A gorgeous hall had been fitted up, under Trippetta's eye, with every kind of device which could possibly give *éclat* to a masquerade. The whole court was in a fever of expectation. As for costumes and characters, it might well be supposed that everybody had come to a decision on such points. Many had made up their minds (as to what *rôles* they should assume) a week, or even a month, in advance; and, in fact, there was not a particle of indecision anywhere—except in the case of the king and his seven ministers. Why *they* hesitated I never could tell, unless they did it by way of a joke. More probably, they found it difficult, on account of being so fat, to make up their minds. At all events, time flew; and, as a last resort, they sent for Trippetta and Hop-Frog.

When the two little friends obeyed the summons of the king, they found him sitting at his wine with the seven members of his cabinet council; but the monarch appeared to be in a very ill humor. He knew that Hop-Frog was not fond of wine; for it excited the poor cripple almost to madness; and madness is no comfortable feeling. But the king loved his practical jokes, and took pleasure in forcing Hop-Frog to drink and (as the king called it) "to be merry."

"Come here, Hop-Frog," said he, as the jester and his friend entered the room; "swallow this bumper to the health of your absent friends [here Hop-Frog sighed] and then let us have the benefit of your invention. We want characters—*characters*, man,—something novel—out of the way. We are wearied with this everlasting sameness. Come, drink! the wine will brighten your wits."

Hop-Frog endeavored, as usual, to get up a jest in reply to these advances from the king; but the effort was too much. It happened to be the poor dwarf's birthday, and the com-

32 mand to drink to his "absent friends" forced the tears to his
eyes. Many large, bitter drops fell into the goblet as he took
it, humbly, from the hand of the tyrant.

"Ah! ha! ha! ha!" roared the latter, as the dwarf reluc-
tantly drained the beaker. "See what a glass of good wine
can do! Why, your eyes are shining already!"

Poor fellow! his large eyes *gleamed*, rather than shone; for
the effect of wine on his excitable brain was not more powerful than instantaneous. He placed the goblet nervously on the
table, and looked around upon the company with a half-
insane stare. They all seemed highly amused at the success
of the king's "*joke.*"

"And now to business," said the prime minister, a *very* fat
man.

"Yes," said the king. "Come, Hop-Frog, lend us your
assistance. Characters, my fine fellow; we stand in need of
characters—all of us—ha! ha! ha!" and as this was seriously
meant for a joke, his laugh was chorused by the seven.

Hop-Frog also laughed, although feebly and somewhat
vacantly.

"Come, come," said the king, impatiently, "have you nothing to suggest?"

"I am endeavoring to think of something *novel*," replied
the dwarf, abstractedly, for he was quite bewildered by the
wine.

"Endeavoring!" cried the tyrant, fiercely; "what do you
mean by *that?* Ah, I perceive. You are sulky, and want more
wine. Here, drink this!" and he poured out another goblet
full and offered it to the cripple, who merely gazed at it,
gasping for breath.

"Drink, I say!" shouted the monster, "or by the fiends—"

The dwarf hesitated. The king grew purple with rage. The

courtiers smirked. Trippetta, pale as a corpse, advanced to the monarch's seat, and falling on her knees before him, implored him to spare her friend.

The tyrant regarded her, for some moments, in evident wonder at her audacity. He seemed quite at a loss what to do or say—how most becomingly to express his indignation. At last, without uttering a syllable, he pushed her violently from him, and threw the contents of the brimming goblet in her face.

The poor girl got up as best she could, and, not daring even to sigh, resumed her position at the foot of the table.

There was a dead silence for about half a minute, during which the falling of a leaf, or of a feather, might have been heard. It was interrupted by a low, but harsh and protracted *grating* sound which seemed to come at once from every corner of the room.

"What—what—*what* are you making the noise for?" demanded the king, turning furiously to the dwarf.

The latter seemed to have recovered, in great measure, from his intoxication, and looking fixedly but quietly into the tyrant's face, merely ejaculated:

"I—I? How could it have been me?"

"The sound appeared to come from without," observed one of the courtiers. "I fancy it was the parrot at the window, whetting his bill upon his cage-wires."

"True," replied the monarch, as if much relieved by the suggestion; "but, on the honor of a knight, I could have sworn that it was the gritting of this vagabond's teeth."

Hereupon the dwarf laughed (the king was too confirmed a joker to object to any one's laughing), and displayed a set of large, powerful, and very repulsive teeth. Moreover, he avowed his perfect willingness to swallow as much wine as

34 desired. The monarch was pacified; and having drained another bumper with no very perceptible ill effect, Hop-Frog entered at once, and with spirit, into the plans for the masquerade.

"I cannot tell what was the association of ideas," observed he, very tranquilly, and as if he had never tasted wine in his life, "but *just after* your majesty had struck the girl and thrown the wine in her face—*just after* your majesty had done this, and while the parrot was making that odd noise outside the window, there came into my mind a capital diversion—one of my own country frolics—often enacted among us, at our masquerades: but here it will be new altogether. Unfortunately, however, it requires a company of eight persons, and——"

"Here we *are!*" cried the king, laughing at his acute discovery of the coincidence; "eight to a fraction—I and my seven ministers. Come! what is the diversion?"

"We call it," replied the cripple, "the Eight Chained Ourang-Outangs, and it really is excellent sport if well enacted."

"*We* will enact it," remarked the king, drawing himself up, and lowering his eyelids.

"The beauty of the game," continued Hop-Frog, "lies in the fright it occasions among the women."

"Capital!" roared in chorus the monarch and his ministry.

"I will equip you as ourang-outangs," proceeded the dwarf; "leave all that to me. The resemblance shall be so striking, that the company of masqueraders will take you for real beasts—and of course, they will be as much terrified as astonished."

"Oh, this is exquisite!" exclaimed the king. "Hop-Frog! I will make a man of you."

"The chains are for the purpose of increasing the confusion by their jangling. You are supposed to have escaped, *en masse,* from your keepers. Your majesty cannot conceive the *effect* produced, at a masquerade, by eight chained ourang-outangs, imagined to be real ones by most of the company; and rushing in with savage cries, among the crowd of delicately and gorgeously habited men and women. The *contrast* is inimitable."

"It *must* be," said the king: and the council arose hurriedly (as it was growing late), to put in execution the scheme of Hop-Frog.

His mode of equipping the party as ourang-outangs was very simple, but effective enough for his purposes. The animals in question had, at the epoch of my story, very rarely been seen in any part of the civilized world; and as the imitations made by the dwarf were sufficiently beast-like and more than sufficiently hideous, their truthfulness to nature was thus thought to be secured.

The king and his ministers were first encased in tight-fitting stockinet shirts and drawers. They were then saturated with tar. At this stage of the process, some of the party suggested feathers; but the suggestion was at once overruled by the dwarf, who soon convinced the eight, by ocular demonstration, that the hair of such a brute as the ourang-outang was much more efficiently represented by *flax.* A thick coating of the latter was accordingly plastered upon the coating of tar. A long chain was now procured. First, it was passed about the waist of the king, and *tied;* then about another of the party, and also tied; then about all successively, in the same manner. When this chaining arrangement was complete, and the party stood as far apart from each other as possible, they formed a circle; and to make all things appear

36 natural, Hop-Frog passed the residue of the chain, in two diameters, at right angles, across the circle, after the fashion adopted, at the present day, by those who capture chimpanzees, or other large apes, in Borneo.

The grand saloon in which the masquerade was to take place, was a circular room, very lofty, and receiving the light of the sun only through a single window at top. At night (the season for which the apartment was especially designed) it was illuminated principally by a large chandelier, depending by a chain from the center of the sky-light, and lowered, or elevated, by means of a counterbalance as usual; but (in order not to look unsightly) this latter passed outside the cupola and over the roof.

The arrangements of the room had been left to Trippetta's superintendence; but, in some particulars, it seems, she had been guided by the calmer judgment of her friend the dwarf. At his suggestion it was that, on this occasion, the chandelier was removed. Its waxen drippings (which, in weather so warm, it was quite impossible to prevent) would have been seriously detrimental to the rich dresses of the guests, who, on account of the crowded state of the saloon, could not *all* be expected to keep from out its centre—that is to say, from under the chandelier. Additional sconces were set in various parts of the hall, out of the way; and a flambeau, emitting sweet odor, was placed in the right hand of each of the Caryatides that stood against the wall—some fifty or sixty all together.

The eight ourang-outangs, taking Hop-Frog's advice, waited patiently until midnight (when the room was thoroughly filled with masqueraders) before making their appearance. No sooner had the clock ceased striking, however, than they rushed, or rather rolled in, all together—for the impediments of their chains caused most of the party to fall, and all to stumble as they entered.

The excitement among the masqueraders was prodigious, and filled the heart of the king with glee. As had been antici- pated, there were not a few of the guests who supposed the ferocious-looking creatures to be beasts of *some* kind in reality, if not precisely ourang-outangs. Many of the women swooned with affright; and had not the king taken the pre- caution to exclude all weapons from the saloon, his party might soon have expiated their frolic in their blood. As it was, a general rush was made for the doors; but the king had ordered them to be locked immediately upon his entrance; and, at the dwarf's suggestion, the keys had been deposited with *him*.

While the tumult was at its height, and each masquerader attentive only to his own safety (for, in fact, there was much *real* danger from the pressure of the excited crowd), the chain by which the chandelier ordinarily hung, and which had been drawn up on its removal, might have been seen very gradually to descend, until its hooked extremity came within three feet of the floor.

Soon after this, the king and his seven friends having reeled about the hall in all directions, found themselves, at length, in its center, and, of course, in immediate contact with the chain. While they were thus situated, the dwarf, who had followed noiselessly at their heels, inciting them to keep up the commotion, took hold of their own chain at the intersection of the two portions which crossed the circle diametrically and at right angles. Here, with the rapidity of thought, he inserted the hook from which the chandelier had been wont to depend; and, in an instant, by some unseen agency, the chandelier-chain was drawn so far upward as

38   to take the hook out of reach, and, as an inevitable consequence, to drag the ourang-outangs together in close connection, and face to face.

The masqueraders, by this time, had recovered, in some measure, from their alarm; and, beginning to regard the whole matter as a well-contrived pleasantry, set up a loud shout of laughter at the predicament of the apes.

"Leave them to *me!*" now screamed Hop-Frog, his shrill voice making itself easily heard through all the din. "Leave them to *me*. I fancy *I* know them. If I can only get a good look at them, *I* can soon tell who they are."

Here, scrambling over the heads of the crowd, he managed to get to the wall; when, seizing a flambeau from one of the Caryatides, he returned, as he went, to the center of the room—leaped, with the agility of a monkey, upon the king's head—and thence clambered a few feet up the chain—holding down the torch to examine the group of ourang-outangs, and still screaming: "*I* shall soon find out who they are!"

And now, while the whole assembly (the apes included) were convulsed with laughter, the jester suddenly uttered a shrill whistle; when the chain flew violently up for about thirty feet—dragging with it the dismayed and struggling ourang-outangs, and leaving them suspended in mid-air between the sky-light and the floor. Hop-Frog, clinging to the chain as it rose, still maintained his relative position in respect to the eight maskers, and still (as if nothing were the matter) continued to thrust his torch down toward them, as though endeavoring to discover who they were.

So thoroughly astonished was the whole company at this ascent, that a dead silence, of about a minute's duration, ensued. It was broken by just such a low, harsh, *grating* sound, as had before attracted the attention of the king and his councillors when the former threw the wine in the face of Trippetta. But, on the present occasion, there could be no question as to *whence* the sound issued. It came from the fang-like teeth of the dwarf, who ground them and gnashed them as he foamed at the mouth, and glared, with an expression of maniacal rage, into the upturned countenances of the king and his seven companions.

"Ah, ha!" said at length the infuriated jester. "Ah, ha! I begin to see who these people *are*, now!" Here, pretending to scrutinize the king more closely, he held the flambeau to the flaxen coat which enveloped him, and which instantly burst into a sheet of vivid flame. In less than half a minute the whole eight ourang-outrangs were blazing fiercely, amid the shrieks of the multitude who gazed at them from below, horror-stricken, and without the power to render them the slightest assistance.

At length the flames, suddenly increasing in virulence, forced the jester to climb higher up the chain, to be out of their reach; and, as he made this movement, the crowd again sank, for a brief instant, into silence. The dwarf seized his opportunity, and once more spoke:

"I now see *distinctly*," he said, "what manner of people these maskers are. They are a great king and his seven privy-councillors,—a king who does not scruple to strike a defense-less girl, and his seven councillors who abet him in the outrage. As for myself, I am simply Hop-Frog, the jester—and *this is my last jest.*"

Owing to the high combustibility of both the flax and the tar to which it adhered, the dwarf had scarcely made an end of his brief speech before the work of vengeance was complete. The eight corpses swung in their chains, a fetid, black-

40 ened, hideous, and indistinguishable mass. The cripple hurled his torch at them, clambered leisurely to the ceiling, and disappeared through the sky-light.

It is supposed that Trippetta, stationed on the roof of the saloon, had been the accomplice of her friend in his fiery revenge, and that, together, they effected their escape to their own country; for neither was seen again.

About the Author

One of the greatest of American writers, Edgar Allan Poe (1809–1849) lived a short, unhappy, and strange life. As a boy he was brilliant in his studies and in athletics. He was reared by a strict foster father (his parents having died when he was two) who took him out of the University of Virginia because Edgar had been drinking and gambling. He got another chance, this time at West Point, but deliberately arranged to be expelled because he disliked the school so much. Disowned by his foster father, Poe worked as an editor and critic for magazines. He married a much younger cousin, but he couldn't get himself settled. When his wife died at the age of twenty-four, Poe became still more unstable and tortured in mind. His stories and poems were attracting much attention, but Poe himself drifted and finally died a miserable death at the age of forty.

"Hop-Frog" is typical of Poe's work—tightly written, intense, exciting.

FOR DISCUSSION

Edgar Allan Poe prided himself on his talent for creating an overpowering emotional atmosphere in his stories. His tales are memorable perhaps more for the emotions or feelings they arouse than for their plots or characters.

Stories in which the emotional atmosphere is of central importance are often called stories of *mood*. Mood is the term applied to the feelings—whether they be feelings of horror, sadness, joy, fun, or any other—which seem to arise from, run through, and surround the story. You probably recognized the mood of "Hop-Frog," climaxed in the events of the masquerade scene, to be one of developing horror.

The following questions should help you to appreciate Poe's skill in creating and developing the mood of this story.

Understanding the Mood

1. This story of horror begins with a description of a king and his ministers, to whom joking and fun were important. Joking and fun seem far removed from horror.

   Consider the king's sense of humor and the description of what kinds of things amused him. If Poe wanted to write a real horror story, do you think this was a good way to begin? Support your answer.

2. The events that immediately preceded Hop-Frog's announcement of his plan for the masquerade, and the announcement itself, are so described by Poe as to give most readers a strong feeling that dreadful things are to come. In describing each event what did Poe specifically do that created the feeling of dread?

3. Try to recall your impressions as you first read the description of the manner in which Hop-Frog clothed and arranged the king and his ministers to resemble ourang-outangs. Which parts of that description led you to guess that something horrible was planned?

   Do you see anything fitting in the selection of ourang-outangs as the masquerade appearance of the king and his ministers?

4. Did you notice Poe's very careful description of the lighting of the hall and the changes made in the position

of the chandelier? If you were reading carefully, this too should have hinted at what would happen.

What hints were in this description?

5. An effective method of emphasizing or highlighting an effect is contrast. If, for example, you wanted to make the whiteness of an object stand out, what kind of background would you provide—a dark or a light one?

In this story, Poe, of course, wanted to highlight the effect of horror. Can you find a contrasting feeling which Poe keeps running through the story up to the *climax*, or most exciting point, in order to make the horror greater? It will help if you will look back at the first part of the story, at the king's reaction when he heard Hop-Frog's plan, and at the mood of the "apes" during the first stages of the masquerade.

What is the contrasting device that Poe used to make the horror even more horrible?

6. In the climactic final stage of Hop-Frog's revenge, Poe's masterful use of powerfully descriptive words contributes considerably to the effect of horror. Select, in the order in which they appear, five or six sentences from the last six paragraphs in which the horror is especially well conveyed through Poe's use of vivid words.

Be prepared to identify these words and to explain their special effect.

7. Sometimes a horror story leaves the reader simply and purely horrified. Sometimes the horror may have been softened by other aspects of the story.

Which statement describes your own reaction to this story? In either case, explain why.

VOCABULARY GROWTH

Using Word Parts to Unlock Meaning

A knowledge of common prefixes in our language can enable you to guess intelligently at the meaning of new

words you meet, especially when there is something in the
rest of the word with which you are familiar.

Two common prefixes which appeared often in this
story were *in* (and its variant *il*) and *pre*. You are probably
aware that *in* often means "not" or "non" as in *insane* or
inability. You probably also know that *pre* means "before,"
as in *predict* or *prejudge*.

But did you know what these italicized words meant
when you met them in the story?

1. *"inimitable jokers"* (page 28)

2. *"illimitable amusement"* (page 29)

3. "not a particle of *indecision*" (page 31)

4. "the contrast is *inimitable*" (page 35)

5. "an *indistinguishable mass*" (page 40)

6. "something in fat which *predisposes* to a joke" (page 28)

7. "had not taken the *precaution* to exclude all weapons"
   (page 37)

To guess intelligently at the meaning, it helps to look
closely at the prefix, at the rest of the word, and at the
phrase or sentence in which it appears.

1. *inimitable* contains *in* (not) + *imitable* (from *imitate*)

2. *illimitable* contains *il* (not) + *limitable* (from *limit*)

3. *predisposes* contains *pre* (before) + *disposes*

4. *precaution* contains *pre* (before) + *caution*

Now look back at the italicized word in each quotation
and try to figure out its meaning.

FOR COMPOSITION

1. Have you ever known a person with a twisted, mean
   sense of humor? If so, tell about him, giving one or two
   examples of his peculiar ideas of what is funny.

2. Nowhere in "Hop-Frog" does the author tell the
   thoughts of the main character. Imagine that you are
   Hop-Frog. The king and his ministers have just forced

44 you to drink the wine. The king has struck Trippetta. Write a composition in which you tell your thoughts. It might begin something like this:

How I hate that monster and his ministers!

3. Horror stories, when they are well written, give the reader pleasure. Use your imagination and see if you can create a short horror story. In writing it, try to make it exciting by using striking, vivid words, as Poe did.

The Summer of the Beautiful White Horse

WILLIAM SAROYAN

Everybody remembers some period of his
childhood which seemed to be a wildly happy
time. Here is a story of two boys who
loved horses, and of the strange
events of a happy summer in their lives.

ONE DAY back there in the good old days when I
was nine and the world was full of every imaginable kind
of magnificence, and life was still a delightful and mysterious
dream, my cousin Mourad, who was considered crazy by
everybody who knew him except me, came to my house at
four in the morning and woke me up by tapping on the
window of my room.

Aram, he said.

I jumped out of bed and looked out the window.

I couldn't believe what I saw.

46   It wasn't morning yet, but it was summer and with day-break not many minutes around the corner of the world it was light enough for me to know I wasn't dreaming.

My cousin Mourad was sitting on a beautiful white horse.

I stuck my head out of the window and rubbed my eyes.

Yes, he said in Armenian. It's a horse. You're not dreaming. Make it quick if you want to ride.

I knew my cousin Mourad enjoyed being alive more than anybody else who had ever fallen into the world by mistake, but this was more than even I could believe.

In the first place, my earliest memories had been memories of horses and my first longings had been longings to ride.

This was the wonderful part.

In the second place, we were poor.

This was the part that wouldn't permit me to believe what I saw.

We were poor. We had no money. Our whole tribe was poverty-stricken. Every branch of the Garoghlanian family was living in the most amazing and comical poverty in the world. Nobody could understand where we ever got money enough to keep us with food in our bellies, not even the old men of the family. Most important of all, though, we were famous for our honesty. We had been famous for our honesty for something like eleven centuries, even when we had been the wealthiest family in what we liked to think was the world. We were proud first, honest next, and after that we believed in right and wrong. None of us would take advantage of anybody in the world, let alone steal.

Consequently, even though I could *see* the horse, so magnificent; even though I could *smell* it, so lovely; even though

I could *hear* it breathing, so exciting; I couldn't *believe* the horse had anything to do with my cousin Mourad or with me or with any of the other members of our family, asleep or awake, because I *knew* my cousin Mourad couldn't have *bought* the horse, and if he couldn't have bought it he must have *stolen* it, and I refused to believe he had stolen it.

No member of the Garoghlanian family could be a thief.

I stared first at my cousin and then at the horse. There was a pious stillness and humor in each of them which on the one hand delighted me and on the other frightened me.

Mourad, I said, where did you steal this horse?

Leap out of the window, he said, if you want to ride.

It was true, then. He *had* stolen the horse. There was no question about it. He had come to invite me to ride or not, as I chose.

Well, it seemed to me stealing a horse for a ride was not the same thing as stealing something else, such as money. For all I knew, maybe it wasn't stealing at all. If you were crazy about horses the way my cousin Mourad and I were, it wasn't stealing. It wouldn't become stealing until we offered to sell the horse, which of course I knew we would never do.

Let me put on some clothes, I said.

All right, he said, but hurry.

I leaped into my clothes.

I jumped down to the yard from the window and leaped up onto the horse behind my cousin Mourad.

That year we lived at the edge of town, on Walnut Avenue. Behind our house was the country: vineyards, orchards, irrigation ditches, and country roads. In less than three minutes we were on Olive Avenue, and then the horse began to trot. The air was new and lovely to breathe. The

48 feel of the horse running was wonderful. My cousin Mourad who was considered one of the craziest members of our family began to sing. I mean, he began to roar.

Every family has a crazy streak in it somewhere, and my cousin Mourad was considered the natural descendant of the crazy streak in our tribe. Before him was our uncle Khosrove, an enormous man with a powerful head of black hair and the largest mustache in the San Joaquin Valley, a man so furious in temper, so irritable, so impatient that he stopped anyone from talking by roaring, *It is no harm; pay no attention to it.*

That was all, no matter what anybody happened to be talking about. Once it was his own son Arak running eight blocks to the barber shop where his father was having his mustache trimmed to tell him their house was on fire. This man Khosrove sat up in the chair and roared, It is no harm; pay no attention to it. The barber said, But the boy says your house is on fire. So Khosrove roared, Enough, it is no harm, I say.

My cousin Mourad was considered the natural descendant of this man, although Mourad's father was Zorab, who was practical and nothing else. That's how it was in our tribe. A man could be the father of his son's flesh, but that did not mean that he was also the father of his spirit. The distribution of the various kinds of spirit of our tribe had been from the beginning capricious and vagrant.

We rode and my cousin Mourad sang. For all anybody knew we were still in the old country where, at least according to some of our neighbors, we belonged. We let the horse run as long as it felt like running.

At last my cousin Mourad said, Get down. I want to ride alone.

Will you let me ride alone? I said.

That is up to the horse, my cousin said. Get down.

The *horse* will let me ride, I said.

We shall see, he said. Don't forget that I have a way with a horse.

Well, I said, any way you have with a horse, I have also.

For the sake of your safety, he said, let us hope so. Get down.

All right, I said, but remember you've got to let me try to ride alone.

I got down and my cousin Mourad kicked his heels into the horse and shouted, *Vazire*, run. The horse stood on its hind legs, snorted, and burst into a fury of speed that was the loveliest thing I had ever seen. My cousin Mourad raced the horse across a field of dry grass to an irrigation ditch, crossed the ditch on the horse, and five minutes later returned, dripping wet.

The sun was coming up.

Now it's my turn to ride, I said.

My cousin Mourad got off the horse.

Ride, he said.

I leaped to the back of the horse and for a moment knew the awfulest fear imaginable. The horse did not move.

Kick into his muscles, my cousin Mourad said. What are you waiting for? We've got to take him back before everybody in the world is up and about.

I kicked into the muscles of the horse. Once again it reared and snorted. Then it began to run. I didn't know what to do. Instead of running across the field to the irrigation ditch the horse ran down the road to the vineyard of Dikran Halabian where it began to leap over vines. The horse leaped over seven vines before I fell. Then it continued running.

My cousin Mourad came running down the road.

I'm not worried about you, he shouted. We've got to get that horse. You go this way and I'll go this way. If you come upon him, be kindly. I'll be near.

I continued down the road and my cousin Mourad went across the field toward the irrigation ditch.

It took him half an hour to find the horse and bring him back.

All right, he said, jump on. The whole world is awake now.

What will we do? I said.

Well, he said, we'll either take him back or hide him until tomorrow morning.

He didn't sound worried and I knew he'd hide him and not take him back. Not for a while, at any rate.

Where will we hide him? I said.

I know a place, he said.

How long ago did you steal this horse? I said.

It suddenly dawned on me that he had been taking these early morning rides for some time and had come for me this morning only because he knew how much I longed to ride.

Who said anything about stealing a horse? he said.

Anyhow, I said, how long ago did you begin riding every morning?

Not until this morning, he said.

Are you telling the truth? I said.

Of course not, he said, but if we are found out, that's what you're to say. I don't want both of us to be liars. All you know is that we started riding this morning.

All right, I said.

He walked the horse quietly to the barn of a deserted vineyard which at one time had been the pride of a farmer named Fetvajian. There were some oats and dry alfalfa in the barn.

We began walking home.

It wasn't easy, he said, to get the horse to behave so nicely. At first it wanted to run wild, but, as I've told you, I have a way with a horse. I can get it to want to do anything *I* want it to do. Horses understand me.

How do you do it? I said.

I have an understanding with a horse, he said.

Yes, but what sort of an understanding? I said.

A simple and honest one, he said.

Well, I said, I wish I knew how to reach an understanding like that with a horse.

You're still a small boy, he said. When you get to be thirteen you'll know how to do it.

I went home and ate a hearty breakfast.

That afternoon my uncle Khosrove came to our house for coffee and cigarettes. He sat in the parlor, sipping and smoking and remembering the old country. Then another visitor arrived, a farmer named John Byro, an Assyrian who, out of loneliness, had learned to speak Armenian. My mother brought the lonely visitor coffee and tobacco and he rolled a cigarette and sipped and smoked, and then at last, sighing sadly, he said, My white horse which was stolen last month is still gone. I cannot understand it.

My uncle Khosrove became very irritated and shouted, It's no harm. What is the loss of a horse? Haven't we all lost the homeland? What is this crying over a horse?

That may be all right for you, a city dweller, to say, John Byro said, but what of my surrey? What good is a surrey without a horse?

Pay no attention to it, my uncle Khosrove roared.

I walked ten miles to get here, John Byro said.

You have legs, my uncle Khosrove shouted.

My left leg pains me, the farmer said.

Pay no attention to it, my uncle Khosrove roared.

That horse cost me sixty dollars, the farmer said.

I spit on money, my uncle Khosrove said.

He got up and walked out of the house, slamming the screen door.

My mother explained.

He has a gentle heart, she said. It is simply that he is homesick and such a large man.

The farmer went away and I ran over to my cousin Mourad's house.

He was sitting under a peach tree, trying to repair the hurt wing of a young robin which could not fly. He was talking to the bird.

What is it? he said.

The farmer, John Byro, I said. He visited our house. He wants his horse. You've had it a month. I want you to promise not to take it back until I learn to ride.

It will take you *a year* to learn to ride, my cousin Mourad said.

We could keep the horse a year, I said.

My cousin Mourad leaped to his feet.

What? he roared. Are you inviting a member of the Garoghlanian family to steal? The horse must go back to its true owner.

When? I said.

In six months at the latest, he said.

He threw the bird into the air. The bird tried hard, almost fell twice, but at last flew away, high and straight.

Early every morning for two weeks my cousin Mourad and I took the horse out of the barn of the deserted vineyard where we were hiding it and rode it, and every morning the horse, when it was my turn to ride alone, leaped over grape vines and small trees and threw me and ran away. Nevertheless, I hoped in time to learn to ride the way my cousin Mourad rode.

One morning on the way to Fetvajian's deserted vineyard we ran into the farmer John Byro who was on his way to town.

Let me do the talking, my cousin Mourad said. I have a way with farmers.

Good morning, John Byro, my cousin Mourad said to the farmer.

The farmer studied the horse eagerly.

Good morning, sons of my friends, he said. What is the name of your horse?

My Heart, my cousin Mourad said in Armenian.

A lovely name, John Byro said, for a lovely horse. I could swear it is the horse that was stolen from me many weeks ago. May I look into its mouth?

Of course, Mourad said.

The farmer looked into the mouth of the horse.

Tooth for tooth, he said. I would swear it *is* my horse if I didn't know your parents. The fame of your family for honesty is well known to me. Yet the horse is the twin of my horse. A suspicious man would believe his eyes instead of his heart. Good day, my young friends.

Good day, John Byro, my cousin Mourad said.

Early the following morning we took the horse to John Byro's vineyard and put it in the barn. The dogs followed us around without making a sound.

The dogs, I whispered to my cousin Mourad. I thought they would bark.

They would at somebody else, he said. I have a way with dogs.

54   My cousin Mourad put his arms around the horse, pressed his nose into the horse's nose, patted it, and then we went away.

That afternoon John Byro came to our house in his surrey and showed my mother the horse that had been stolen and returned.

I do not know what to think, he said. The horse is stronger than ever. Better-tempered, too. I thank God.

My uncle Khosrove, who was in the parlor, became irritated and shouted, Quiet, man, quiet. Your horse has been returned. Pay no attention to it.

About the Author

William Saroyan was born in California in 1908 of Armenian immigrant parents. He left junior high school to work at one job after another; none seemed to last. His first published short story attracted nation-wide recognition, and his subsequent stories proved very successful. He has also written several novels, the best known of which is *The Human Comedy*. His play *The Time of Your Life* won the Pulitzer Award in 1940. He wrote the lyrics for "Come On-a My House," which became the number one hit song in the United States.

Like the characters in the story you have read, Mr. Saroyan has certain strange ways about him; he dresses very unconventionally, and he likes the company of "rough-and-ready" people. He is noted, in his own life and in his stories, for the warm sympathy he has for all kinds of people.

FOR DISCUSSION

Understanding the Mood

1. Like "Hop-Frog," this is predominantly a mood story.

   No one word is really adequate to describe the mood of "The Summer of the Beautiful White Horse." Which combination of the following words would you select to describe it? Support your choices by references to the people and events in the story.

nightmarish	joyful	serious	high-spirited
dreamlike	sad	light-hearted	heavy

   As you answer the following questions, keep in mind the words you chose to describe the mood.

2. The title of the story immediately suggests much of the mood. How? *We always wanted to do* *normally the family shared*

3. The *style* (the way in which Mr. Saroyan puts his thoughts into words) of the first sentence and its *content* (the ideas expressed) also help to establish the mood. How do they do so?

4. Mr. Saroyan's style, especially at the beginning, is most unusual. Did you notice the many very short one-sentence paragraphs at the start? Examine these paragraphs. Are they connected in any way with the mood he is trying to establish?

5. Some of the word pictures in the story also help to create and keep up this mood. For example, on pages 48 and 49, the author writes: ". . . even though I could *see* the horse, so magnificent; even though I could *smell* it, so lovely; even though I could *hear* it breathing, so exciting. . . ."

   a. What kind of mood does this picture create?

   b. Find, on the next few pages, other word pictures which carry forward the mood of the story.

6. The author's choice of characters helps to establish and keep up the mood.

   a. Which character is the most important in this regard? What qualities of his personality have this effect?

    b. What other characters in the story help to support the mood? How?

  7. Even the treatment of serious ideas in this story is in keeping with the mood. An important idea in the story is *honesty*. How is the treatment of honesty unusual? How does this treatment fit the mood of the story?

A Closer Look at the Characters

  1. Mourad really did steal. Did you feel like condemning him for his theft? Explain your answer by reference to the events of the story and his total character.

  2. Suppose you had called Mourad a thief because of his actions. How do you suppose he would have answered?

  3. Consider what John Byro said and the way he acted when he found the boys riding his horse. Consider also the words he spoke in the last paragraph. Do you think he was a stupid man or not? Support your answer.

VOCABULARY GROWTH

Learning About the History of Words

    Mr. Saroyan uses simple words in this story. Chances are there were few, if any, words you did not understand.

    Many of the words in the story do, however, illustrate an interesting fact about our language—that so much of our English vocabulary has come down to us from the ancient Romans, directly or indirectly.

    One sentence in the story goes like this: "There was a *pious* stillness and humor in each of them [in Mourad and in the horse]."

    The word *pious* came into English from the French word *piété*. (The English noun is *piety*.) Many of our words came from the French, when an army of Frenchmen from Normandy conquered England in 1066. But the French word came from the Latin (Roman) word *pius*. (A Roman army at a still earlier time had conquered France.) *Pius* in Latin meant "dutiful," "tender," "kind," "respectful."

    Look up the word *pious*. What does it mean in the sentence about Mourad and the horse?

Another sentence in the story reads: "...my cousin Mourad was considered the natural *descendant* of the crazy streak in our tribe."

The word *descendant* came into English from an old French word *descendre*, which in turn came from a Latin (Roman) word composed of two parts: *de*, meaning "down from," and *scandere*, "to climb down."

Today *descend* has other meanings besides "climb down." Can you see what its noun form, *descendant*, means in the sentence about Mourad? And can you see how a word meaning "climb down" eventually developed the meaning it has in the modern word *descendant*?

1. In the sentence below there are two italicized words that come from the Romans. Look them up in a good dictionary that gives origins of words. You will find the history of the first word to be especially interesting; keep in mind that goats by nature seem to behave in the most unexpected and freakish ways. How did this word get its modern meaning? And what does the second word in italics mean in the sentence?

   "The distribution of the various kinds of spirit of our tribe had been...*capricious* and *vagrant*."

2. Look up the origin of *suspicious* and see what connection you can find between its origin and its modern meaning in this sentence from the story:

   "A *suspicious* man would believe his eyes instead of his heart."

FOR COMPOSITION

1. Do you recall a time in your own childhood when one or several events occurred that made you extremely happy? Describe that time and the events that occurred.

2. Did you ever do a wrong thing because it was terribly tempting, and then make up reasons to prove that what you were doing was not really so bad? Write a compo-

sition in which you tell about the temptation, what you did, and how you justified what you did.

3. Do you know anyone whose behavior is odd and eccentric, so that some people consider him "strange" or "crazy"? Describe that person and tell whether you agree with those who think him "strange" or "crazy."

STORIES
OF
THEME

The Bishop's Silver

VICTOR HUGO

A desperate-looking vagabond is roaming the streets of the town. A kindly bishop, who lives very simply, has some valuable silverware in his home. You may be surprised by the turn of events in this story.

JUST AS the bishop entered, Madame Magloire was speaking with some warmth. She was talking to *Mademoiselle* upon a familiar subject, and one to which the bishop was quite accustomed. It was a discussion on the means of fastening the front door.

It seems while Madame Magloire was out making provision for supper, she had heard the news in sundry places. There was talk that an ill-favoured runaway, a suspicious vagabond, had arrived and was lurking somewhere in the town, and that some unpleasant adventures might befall those who should come home late that night; besides, that the police were very bad, as the prefect and the mayor did not like one another, and were hoping to injure each other by untoward events; that it was the part of wise people to be their own police, and to protect their own persons; and that every one ought to be careful to shut up, bolt, and bar his house properly, and *secure his door thoroughly*.

Madame Magloire dwelt upon these last words; but the bishop, having come from a cold room, seated himself before the fire and began to warm himself, and then, he was thinking of something else. He did not hear a word of what was let fall by Madame Magloire, and she repeated it. Then Mademoiselle Baptistine, endeavouring to satisfy Madame Magloire without displeasing her brother, ventured to say timidly:

"Brother, do you hear what Madame Magloire says?"

"I heard something of it indistinctly," said the bishop. Then turning his chair half round, putting his hands on his knees, and raising towards the old servant his cordial and good-humoured face, which the firelight shone upon, he said: "Well, well! what is the matter? Are we in any great danger?"

Then Madame Magloire began her story again, unconsciously exaggerating it a little. It appeared that a barefooted gipsy man, a sort of dangerous beggar, was in the town. He had gone for lodging to Jacquin Labarre, who had refused to receive him; he had been seen to enter the town by the boulevard Gassendi, and to roam through the street at dusk. A man with a knapsack and a rope, and a terrible-looking face.

"Indeed!" said the bishop.

This readiness to question her encouraged Madame Magloire; it seemed to indicate that the bishop was really well-nigh alarmed. She continued triumphantly: "Yes, monseigneur; it is true. There will something happen to-night in the town; everybody says so. The police are so badly organized (a convenient repetition). To live in this mountainous country, and not even to have street lamps! If one goes out, it is dark as a pocket. And I say, monseigneur, and mademoiselle says also—"

"Me?" interrupted the sister; "I say nothing. Whatever my brother does is well done."

Madame Magloire went on as if she had not heard this protestation:

"We say that this house is not safe at all; and if monseigneur will permit me, I will go and tell Paulin Musebois, the locksmith, to come and put the old bolts in the door again; they are there, and it will take but a minute. I say we must have bolts, were it only for to-night; for I say that a door which opens by a latch on the outside to the first comer, nothing could be more horrible: and then monseigneur has the habit of always saying 'Come in,' even at midnight. But, my goodness! there is no need even to ask leave—"

At this moment there was a violent knock on the door.

"Come in!" said the bishop.

THE door opened.

It opened quickly, quite wide, as if pushed by someone boldly and with energy.

A man entered....

He came in, took one step, and paused, leaving the door open behind him. He had his knapsack on his back, his stick in his hand, and a rough, hard, tired, and fierce look in his eyes, as seen by the firelight. He was hideous. It was an apparition of ill omen.

Madame Magloire had not even the strength to scream. She stood trembling with her mouth open.

Mademoiselle Baptistine turned, saw the man enter, and started up half alarmed; then, slowly turning back again towards the fire, she looked at her brother, and her face resumed its usual calmness and serenity.

The bishop looked upon the man with a tranquil eye.

As he was opening his mouth to speak, doubtless to ask the stranger what he wanted, the man, leaning with both hands on his club, glanced from one to another in turn, and without waiting for the bishop to speak, said in a loud voice:

"See here! My name is Jean Valjean. I am a convict; I have been nineteen years in the galleys. Four days ago I was set free, and started for Pontarlier, which is my destination; during those four days I have walked from Toulon. To-day I have walked twelve leagues. When I reached this place this evening I went to an inn, and they sent me away on account of my yellow passport, which I had shown at the mayor's office, as was necessary. I went to another inn; they said: 'Get out!' It was the same with one as with another; nobody would have me. I went to the prison, and the turnkey would not let me in. There in the square I lay down upon a stone; a good woman showed me your house, and said: 'Knock there!' I have knocked. What is this place? Are you an inn? I have money; my savings, one hundred and nine francs and fifteen sous which I have earned in the galleys by my work for nineteen years. I will pay. What do I care? I have money. I am very tired—twelve leagues on foot, and I am so hungry. Can I stay?"

"Madame Magloire," said the bishop, "put on another plate."

The man took three steps, and came near the lamp which stood on the table. "Stop," he exclaimed; as if he had not been understood, "not that, did you understand me? I am a galley-slave—a convict—I am just from the galleys." He

64 drew from his pocket a large sheet of yellow paper, which he unfolded. "There is my passport, yellow as you see. That is enough to have me kicked out wherever I go. Will you read it? I know how to read, I do. I learned in the galleys. There is a school there for those who care for it. See, here is what they have put in the passport: 'Jean Valjean, a liberated convict, native of ———,' you don't care for that, 'has been nineteen years in the galleys; five years for burglary; fourteen years for having attempted four times to escape. This man is very dangerous.' There you have it! Everybody has thrust me out; will you receive me? Is this an inn? Can you give me something to eat, and a place to sleep? Have you a stable?"

"Madame Magloire," said the bishop, "put some sheets on the bed in the alcove."

Madame Magloire went out to fulfil her orders.

The bishop turned to the man:

"Monsieur, sit down and warm yourself: we are going to take supper presently, and your bed will be made ready while you sup."

At last the man quite understood; his face, the expression of which till then had been gloomy and hard, now expressed stupefaction, doubt, and joy, and became absolutely wonderful. He began to stutter like a madman.

"True? What! You will keep me? you won't drive me away? a convict! You call me *Monsieur* and don't say 'Get out, dog!' as everybody else does. I thought that you would send me away, so I told first off who I am. Oh! the fine woman who sent me here! I shall have a supper! a bed like other people with mattress and sheets—a bed! It is nineteen years that I have not slept on a bed. You are really willing that I should stay? You are good people! Besides I have money. I will pay well. I beg your pardon, Monsieur Innkeeper, what is your name? I will pay all you say. You are a fine man. You are an innkeeper, an't you?"

"I am a priest who lives here," said the bishop.

While he was talking, the bishop shut the door, which he had left wide open.

Madame Magloire brought in a plate and set it on the table.

"Madame Magloire," said the bishop, "put this plate as near the fire as you can." Then turning towards his guest, he added: "The night wind is raw in the Alps; you must be cold, Monsieur."

Every time he said this word *monsieur*, with his gently solemn, and heartily hospitable voice, the man's countenance lighted up. *Monsieur*, to a convict, is a glass of water to a man dying of thirst at sea. Ignominy thirsts for respect.

"The lamp," said the bishop, "gives a very poor light."

Madame Magloire understood him, and going to his bed-chamber, took from the mantel the two silver candlesticks, lighted the candles, and placed them on the table.

Meantime she had served up supper; it consisted of soup made of water, oil, bread, and salt, a little pork, a scrap of mutton, a few figs, a green cheese, and a large loaf of rye bread. She had, without asking, added to the usual dinner of the bishop a bottle of fine old Mauves wine.

The bishop's countenance was lighted up with this expression of pleasure, peculiar to hospitable natures. "To supper!" he said briskly, as was his habit when he had a guest. He seated the man at his right. Mademoiselle Baptistine, perfectly quiet and natural, took her place at his left.

The bishop said the blessing, and then served the soup himself, according to his usual custom. The man fell to, eating greedily.

Suddenly the bishop said, "It seems to me something is lacking on the table."

The fact was, that Madame Magloire had set out only the three plates which were necessary. Now it was the custom of the house, when the bishop had any one to supper, to set all six of the silver plates on the table, an innocent display. This graceful appearance of luxury was a sort of childlikeness which was full of charm in this gentle but austere household, which elevated poverty to dignity.

Madame Magloire understood the remark; without a word she went out, and a moment afterwards the three plates for which the bishop had asked were shining on the cloth, symmetrically arranged before each of the three guests. During the meal there were few words spoken. The visitor was plainly weary and it was not long before they made ready for the night.

AFTER having said good-night to his sister, Monseigneur Bienvenu took one of the silver candlesticks from the table, handed the other to his guest, and said to him:

"Monsieur, I will show you to your room."

The man followed him.

The house was so arranged that one could reach the alcove in the oratory only by passing through the bishop's sleeping chamber. Just as they were passing through his room Madame Magloire was putting up the silver in the cupboard at the head of the bed. It was the last thing she did every night before going to bed.

The bishop left his guest in the alcove, before a clean white bed. The man set down the candlestick upon a small table.

"Come," said the bishop, "a good night's rest to you: to-morrow morning, before you go, you shall have a cup of warm milk from our cows."

"Thank you, Monsieur l'Abbé," said the man.

Scarcely had he pronounced these words of peace, when suddenly he made a singular motion which would have chilled the two good women of the house with horror, had they witnessed it. Even now it is hard for us to understand what impulse he obeyed at that moment. Did he intend to give a warning or to throw out a menace? Or was he simply obeying a sort of instinctive impulse, obscure ever to himself? He turned abruptly towards the old man, crossed his arms, and casting a wild look upon his host, exclaimed in a harsh voice:

"Ah, now, indeed! You lodge me in your house, as near you as that!"

He checked himself, and added, with a laugh, in which there was something horrible:

"Have you reflected upon it? Who tells you that I am not a murderer?"

The bishop responded:

"God will take care of that."

Then with gravity, moving his lips like one praying or talking to himself, he raised two fingers of his right hand and blessed the man, who, however, did not bow; and without turning his head or looking behind him, went into his chamber.

When the alcove was occupied, a heavy serge curtain was drawn in the oratory, concealing the altar. Before this curtain the bishop knelt as he passed out, and offered a short prayer.

A moment afterwards he was walking in the garden, surrendering mind and soul to a dreamy contemplation of

68 these grand and mysterious works of God, which night makes visible to the eye.

As to the man, he was so completely exhausted that he did not even avail himself of the clean white sheets; he blew out the candle with his nostril, after the manner of convicts, and fell on the bed, dressed as he was, into a sound sleep.

Midnight struck as the bishop came back to his chamber. A few moments afterwards all in the little house slept. . . .

As the cathedral clock struck two, Jean Valjean awoke. What awakened him was, too good a bed. For nearly twenty years he had not slept in a bed, and, although he had not undressed, the sensation was too novel not to disturb his sleep.

He had slept something more than four hours. His fatigue had passed away. He was not accustomed to give many hours to repose.

He opened his eyes, and looked for a moment into the obscurity about him, then he closed them to go to sleep again.

When many diverse sensations have disturbed the day, when the mind is preoccupied, we can fall asleep once, but not a second time. Sleep comes at first much more readily than it comes again. Such was the case with Jean Valjean. He could not get to sleep again, and so he began to think.

He was in one of those moods in which the ideas we have in our minds are perturbed. There was a kind of vague ebb and flow in his brain. His oldest and latest memories floated about pell mell, and crossed each other confusedly, losing their own shapes, swelling beyond measure, then disappearing all at once, as if in a muddy and troubled stream. Many thoughts came to him, but there was one which continually presented itself, and which drove away all others. What that thought was, we shall tell directly. He had noticed the six silver plates and the large ladle that Madame Magloire had put on the table.

Those six silver plates took possession of him. There they were, within a few steps. At the very moment that he passed through the middle room to reach the one he was now in, the old servant was placing them in a little cupboard at the head of the bed. He had marked that cupboard well: on the right, coming from the dining-room. They were solid; and old silver. With the big ladle, they would bring at least two hundred francs, double what he had got for nineteen year's labour. True; he would have got more if the "*government*" had not "*robbed*" him.

His mind wavered a whole hour, and a long one, in fluctuation and in struggle. The clock struck three. He opened his eyes, rose up hastily in bed, reached out his arm and felt his haversack, which he had put into the corner of the alcove, then he thrust out his legs and placed his feet on the ground, and found himself, he knew not how, seated on his bed.

He remained for some time lost in thought in that attitude, which would have had a rather ominous look, had anyone seen him there in the dusk—he only awake in the slumbering house. All at once he stooped down, took off his shoes, and put them softly upon the mat in front of the bed, then he resumed his thinking posture, and was still again.

In that hideous meditation, the ideas which we have been pointing out, troubled his brain without ceasing, entered, departed, returned, and became a sort of weight upon him; and then he thought, too, he knew not why, and with that mechanical obstinacy that belongs to reverie, of a convict named Brevet, whom he had known in the galleys, and whose

70 trousers were only held up by a single knit cotton suspender. The checked pattern of that suspender came continually before his mind.

He continued in this situation, and would perhaps have remained there until daybreak, if the clock had not struck the quarter or the half-hour. The clock seemed to say to him: "Come along!"

He rose to his feet, hesitated for a moment longer, and listened; all was still in the house; he walked straight and cautiously towards the window, which he could discern. The night was not very dark; there was a full moon, across which large clouds were driving before the wind. This produced alternations of light and shade, out-of-doors eclipses and illuminations, and in-doors a kind of glimmer. This glimmer, enough to enable him to find his way, changing with the passing clouds, resembled that sort of livid light, which falls through the window of a dungeon before which men are passing and repassing. On reaching the window, Jean Valjean examined it. It had no bars, opened into the garden, and was fastened, according to the fashion of the country, with a little wedge only. He opened it; but as the cold, keen air rushed into the room, he closed it again immediately. He looked into the garden with that absorbed look which studies rather than sees. The garden was enclosed with a white wall, quite low, and readily scaled. Beyond, against the sky, he distinguished the tops of trees at equal distances apart, which showed that this wall separated the garden from an avenue or a lane planted with trees.

When he had taken this observation, he turned like a man whose mind is made up, went to his alcove, took his haversack, opened it, fumbled in it, took out something which he laid upon the bed, put his shoes into one of his pockets, tied up his bundle, swung it upon his shoulders, put on his cap, and pulled the vizor down over his eyes, felt for his stick, and went and put it in the corner of the window, then returned to the bed, and resolutely took up the object which he had laid on it. It looked like a short iron bar, pointed at one end like a spear.

It would have been hard to distinguish in the darkness for what use this piece of iron had been made. Could it be a lever? Could it be a club?

In the day-time, it would have been seen to be nothing but a miner's drill. At that time, the convicts were sometimes employed in quarrying stone on the high hills that surround Toulon, and they often had miners' tools in their possession. Miners' drills are of solid iron, terminating at the lower end in a point, by means of which they are sunk into the rock.

He took the drill in his right hand, and holding his breath, with stealthy steps, he moved towards the door of the next room, which was the bishop's, as we know. On reaching the door, he found it unlatched. The bishop had not closed it.

JEAN VALJEAN listened. Not a sound.

He pushed the door.

He pushed it lightly with the end of his finger, with the stealthy and timorous carefulness of a cat. The door yielded to the pressure with a silent, imperceptible movement, which made the opening a little wider.

He waited a moment, and then pushed the door again more boldly.

It yielded gradually and silently. The opening was now wide enough for him to pass through; but there was a small

72 table near the door which with it formed a troublesome angle, and which barred the entrance.

Jean Valjean saw the obstacle. At all hazards the opening must be made still wider.

He so determined, and pushed the door a third time, harder than before. This time a rusty hinge suddenly sent out into the darkness a harsh and prolonged creak.

Jean Valjean shivered. The noise of this hinge sounded in his ears as clear and terrible as the trumpet of the Judgment Day.

In the fantastic exaggeration of the first moment, he almost imagined that this hinge had become animate, and suddenly endowed with a terrible life; and that it was barking like a dog to warn everybody, and rouse the sleepers.

He stopped, shuddering and distracted, and dropped from his tiptoes to his feet. He felt the pulses of his temples beat like trip-hammers, and it appeared to him that his breath came from his chest with the roar of wind from a cavern. It seemed impossible that the horrible sound of this incensed hinge had not shaken the whole house with the shock of an earthquake: the door pushed by him had taken the alarm, and had called out; the old man would arise; the two old women would scream; help would come; in a quarter of an hour the town would be alive with it, and the gendarmes in pursuit. For a moment he thought he was lost.

He stood still, petrified like the pillar of salt, not daring to stir. Some minutes passed. The door was wide open; he ventured a look into the room. Nothing had moved. He listened. Nothing was stirring in the house. The noise of the rusty hinge had wakened nobody.

This first danger was over, but still he felt within him a frightful tumult. Nevertheless he did not flinch. Not even when he thought he was lost had he flinched. His only thought was to make an end of it quickly. He took one step and was in the room.

A deep calm filled the chamber. Here and there indistinct, confused forms could be distinguished; which by day, were papers scattered over a table, open folios, books piled on a stool, an arm-chair with clothes on it, a *prie-dieu,* but now were only dark corners and whitish spots. Jean Valjean advanced, carefully avoiding the furniture. At the further end of the room he could hear the equal and quiet breathing of the sleeping bishop.

Suddenly he stopped: he was near the bed, he had reached it sooner than he thought.

Nature sometimes joins her effects and her appearances to our acts with a sort of serious and intelligent appropriateness, as if she would compel us to reflect. For nearly a half hour a great cloud had darkened the sky. At the moment when Jean Valjean paused before the bed the cloud broke as if purposely, and a ray of moonlight crossing the high window suddenly lighted up the bishop's pale face. He slept tranquilly. He was almost entirely dressed, though in bed, on account of the cold nights of the lower Alps, with a dark woollen garment which covered his arms to the wrists. His head had fallen on the pillow in the unstudied attitude of slumber; over the side of the bed hung his hand, ornamented with the pastoral ring, and which had done so many good deeds, so many pious acts. His entire countenance was lit up with a vague expression of content, hope, and happiness. It was more than a smile and almost a radiance. On his forehead rested the indescribable reflection of an unseen light. The souls of the upright in sleep have vision of a mysterious heaven.

A reflection from this heaven shone upon the bishop.

But it was also a luminous transparency, for this heaven was within him; this heaven was his conscience.

At the instant when the moonbeam overlay, so to speak, this inward radiance, the sleeping bishop appeared as if in a halo. But it was very mild, and veiled in an ineffable twilight. The moon in the sky, nature drowsing, the garden without a pulse, the quiet house, the hour, the moment, the silence, added something strangely solemn and unutterable to the venerable repose of this man, and enveloped his white locks and his closed eyes with a serene and majestic glory, this face where all was hope and confidence—this old man's head and infant's slumber.

There was something of divinity almost in this man, thus unconsciously august.

Jean Valjean was in the shadow with the iron drill in his hand, erect, motionless, terrified, at this radiant figure. He had never seen anything comparable to it. This confidence filled him with fear. The moral world has no greater spectacle than this; a troubled and restless conscience on the verge of committing an evil deed, contemplating the sleep of a good man.

He did not remove his eyes from the old man. The only thing which was plain from his attitude and his countenance was a strange indecision. You would have said he was hesitating between two realms, that of the doomed and that of the saved. He appeared ready either to cleave this skull, or to kiss this hand.

In a few moments he raised his left hand slowly to his forehead and took off his hat; then, letting his hand fall with the same slowness, Jean Valjean resumed his contemplations, his cap in his left hand, his club in his right, and his hair bristling on his fierce-looking head.

Under this frightful gaze the bishop still slept in profoundest peace.

The crucifix above the mantelpiece was dimly visible in the moonlight, apparently extending its arms towards both, with a benediction for one and a pardon for the other.

Suddenly Jean Valjean put on his cap, then passed quickly, without looking at the bishop, along the bed, straight to the cupboard which he perceived near its head; he raised the drill to force the lock; the key was in it; he opened it; the first thing he saw was the basket of silver, he took it, crossed the room with hasty stride, careless of noise, reached the door, entered the oratory, took his stick, stepped out, put the silver in his knapsack, threw away the basket, ran across the garden, leaped over the wall like a tiger, and fled.

THE next day at sunrise, Monseigneur Bienvenu was walking in the garden. Madame Magloire ran towards him quite beside herself.

"Monseigneur, monseigneur," cried she, "does your greatness know where the silver basket is?"

"Yes," said the bishop.

"God be praised!" said she, "I did not know what had become of it."

The bishop had just found the basket on a flower-bed. He gave it to Madame Magloire and said: "There it is."

"Yes," said she, "but there is nothing in it. The silver?"

"Ah!" said the bishop, "it is the silver then that troubles you. I do not know where that is."

"Good heavens! it is stolen. That man who came last night stole it."

And in the twinkling of an eye, with all the agility of which her age was capable, Madame Magloire ran to the oratory, went into the alcove, and came back to the bishop. The bishop was bending with some sadness over a cochlearia des Guillons, which the basket had broken in falling. He looked up at Madame Magloire's cry:

"Monseigneur, the man has gone! the silver is stolen!"

While she was uttering this exclamation her eyes fell on an angle of the garden where she saw traces of an escalade. A capstone of the wall had been thrown down.

"See, there is where he got out; he jumped into Cochefilet lane. The abominable fellow! he has stolen our silver!"

The bishop was silent for a moment, then raising his serious eyes, he said mildly to Madame Magloire:

"Now first, did this silver belong to us?"

Madame Magloire did not answer; after a moment the bishop continued:

"Madame Magloire, I have for a long time wrongfully withheld this silver; it belonged to the poor. Who was this man? A poor man evidently."

"Alas! alas!" returned Madame Magloire. "It is not on my account or mademoiselle's; it is all the same to us. But it is on yours, monseigneur. What is monseigneur going to eat from now?"

The bishop looked at her with amazement:

"How so! have we no tin plates?"

Madame Magloire shrugged her shoulders.

"Tin smells."

"Well, then, iron plates."

Madame Magloire made an expressive gesture.

"Iron tastes."

"Well," said the bishop, "then, wooden plates."

In a few minutes he was breakfasting at the same table at which Jean Valjean sat the night before. While breakfast-

ing, Monseigneur Bienvenu pleasantly remarked to his sister
who said nothing, and Madame Magloire who was grumbling
to herself, that there was really no need even of a wooden
spoon or fork to dip a piece of bread into a cup of milk.

"Was there ever such an idea?" said Madame Magloire
to herself, as she went backwards and forwards: "to take
in a man like that, and to give him a bed beside him; and yet
what a blessing it was that he did nothing but steal! Oh, my
stars! it makes the chills run over me when I think of it!"

Just as the brother and sister were rising from the table,
there was a knock at the door.

"Come in," said the bishop.

The door opened. A strange, fierce group appeared on
the threshold. Three men were holding a fourth by the
collar. The three men were gendarmes; the fourth Jean
Valjean.

A brigadier of gendarmes, who appeared to head the
group, was near the door. He advanced towards the bishop,
giving a military salute.

"Monseigneur," said he—

At this word Jean Valjean, who was sullen and seemed
entirely cast down, raised his head with a stupefied air—

"Monseigneur!" he murmured, "then it is not the curé!"

"Silence!" said a gendarme, "it is monseigneur, the
bishop."

In the meantime Monseigneur Bienvenu had approached
as quickly as his great age permitted:

"Ah, there you are!" said he, looking towards Jean Valjean, "I am glad to see you. But! I gave you the candlesticks
also, which are silver like the rest, and would bring two
hundred francs. Why did you not take them along with your
plates?"

78   Jean Valjean opened his eyes and looked at the bishop with an expression which no human tongue could describe.

"Monseigneur," said the brigadier, "then what this man said was true? We met him. He was going like a man who was running away, and we arrested him in order to see. He had this silver."

"And he told you," interrupted the bishop, with a smile, "that it had been given him by a good old priest with whom he had passed the night. I see it all. And you brought him back here? It is all a mistake."

"If that is so," said the brigadier, "we can let him go."

"Certainly," replied the bishop.

The gendarmes released Jean Valjean, who shrank back—

"Is it true that they let me go?" he said in a voice almost inarticulate, as if he were speaking in his sleep.

"Yes! you can go. Do you not understand?" said a gendarme.

"My friend," said the bishop, "before you go away, here are your candlesticks; take them."

He went to the mantelpiece, took the two candlesticks, and brought them to Jean Valjean. The two women beheld the action without a word, or gesture, or look, that might disturb the bishop.

Jean Valjean was trembling in every limb. He took the two candlesticks mechanically, and with a wild appearance.

"Now," said the bishop, "go in peace. By the way, my friend, when you come again, you need not come through the garden. You can always come in and go out by the front door. It is closed only with a latch, day or night."

Then turning to the gendarmes, he said:

"Messieurs, you can retire." The gendarmes withdrew.

Jean Valjean felt like a man who is just about to faint.

The bishop approached him, and said, in a low voice:

"Forget not, never forget that you have promised me to use this silver to become an honest man."

Jean Valjean, who had no recollection of this promise, stood confounded. The bishop had laid much stress upon these words as he uttered them. He continued, solemnly:

"Jean Valjean, my brother: you belong no longer to evil, but to good. It is your soul that I am buying for you. I withdraw it from dark thoughts and from the spirit of perdition, and I give it to God!"

About the Author

Victor Hugo is one of the great names in French literature. He was born in 1802; his father was a general in Napoleon's army. A volume of poetry which he published at the age of twenty won him national acclaim and a pension from the king. Later he became the leader of a revolutionary movement in literature and his plays were read and performed all over Europe. His interest in poor people and the underdog resulted in political activity against the French government, and Hugo was exiled from France. In England he wrote his masterpiece, the novel *Les Misérables,* from which "The Bishop's Silver" is taken. When the French government changed in 1870, Victor Hugo returned to his native country. He never lost his interest in the depressed lower classes, an interest evident in the story you have just finished reading.

FOR DISCUSSION

Understanding the Characters

1. Very few people would have welcomed a man of Jean Valjean's appearance and reputation as the bishop did. How would you have behaved if Jean Valjean had come to your door with his story? What details of his appearance, his manner of speaking, and his history would have made you react this way?

2. In considering all of Jean Valjean's behavior in the first part of the story, before he fell asleep, do you feel any trace of sympathy for him, or none at all? Review what he said and what he did in order to provide evidence to justify your answer.

3. Now consider your first impressions of the bishop. The author never *tells* what kind of person he is. He lets the reader draw his own conclusions. What conclusions about the bishop's character can you draw from the first parts of the story? Consider the following:

   a. How much talking does he do? What does he say?

   b. How does he describe himself when Jean Valjean asks, " 'You are an innkeeper, an't you?' " Why doesn't he tell the whole truth about his rank in the Church? (He is a very high and respected official of the Roman Catholic Church.)

   c. How luxurious is the food which is served in his house?

   d. What attitude does he seem to have toward the criminal, Jean Valjean?

4. When Jean Valjean wakes from his sleep, the author tells us that "His *oldest* and *latest* memories ... crossed each other confusedly. ..." What kind of memories do you suppose these were?

   Some explanation of how Valjean feels toward the world is offered on page 69 in this sentence: "True, he would have got more [money] if the *'government'* had not *'robbed'* him." What conflict do you think must be going on in his mind?

5. What is your explanation of the fact that Jean Valjean stole the silver from the very man who had befriended him so? Did the bishop's friendship have no effect on him? A good explanation of his decision to steal will show that the reasons why people perform certain actions may often be very complicated.

6. When Madame Magloire discovers the theft, the bishop makes certain odd statements about the ownership of the silver and the use of eating utensils. What is his real meaning?

   Do his statements surprise you? Explain your answer.

7. When Jean Valjean is brought in by the gendarmes, the bishop continues to shock us by his strange behavior.

   Are his "white lie" and his offer of the silver candlesticks consistent or inconsistent with his character as we know it? Why?

8. We are told that Jean Valjean "shrank back," "was trembling," and "felt like a man who is about to faint"; not when he was caught by the gendarmes, but when he was released. How do you explain his reacting this way at this particular moment?

   There will undoubtedly be more "confused" thoughts in Jean Valjean's mind when he leaves the bishop's home. What guess would you make as to what these thoughts will be?

Understanding the Theme

The sequence of events that make up the action of a story is the *plot* of the story. The *theme* of a story is not the plot. It is the underlying idea, the message, the particular truth about the world, or about human character, or about life or human society, which the author wants to convey to his readers. In most stories, the theme arises out of the events of the story—the plot—and out of the *interaction* of the characters in the story. (Interaction means the manner in which the characters act toward one another and influence one another.) If you will consider the questions which follow, you will be helped to understand what ideas Victor Hugo, the author, wanted to convey in "The Bishop's Silver" about such problems as these:

a. What are some of the factors which turn people toward wrongdoing?

b. What is the responsibility of people in high position toward others less fortunate?

c. What attitude ought one to have toward those who have done wrong?

1. This story is part of a novel by Victor Hugo, called *Les Misérables*. The French title is close enough to English so that you can make a good guess as to the meaning. Jean Valjean is one of "the miserable ones," representing others like him in the world. He was not always a criminal.

What do his descriptions of himself and his past, on pages 63 and 64, tell you about the kind of people he is supposed to represent in the story? Note, for example, his statement. " 'Everybody has thrust me out.' " What guess would you make about the conditions Valjean must have lived in when he was younger?

2. The bishop's servant, Madame Magloire, probably represents most ordinary people in their reaction to men like Jean Valjean. How would you describe that reaction as it is indicated in the opening pages of the story and later, when she discovers the theft of the silver?

3. The bishop's attitude contrasts with Madame Magloire's. What differences did you observe?

4. The bishop seems to have some strange ideas about property. Where did he express them? What did he mean? Consider, in this connection, his last gift of the two silver candlesticks to the thief, Valjean. Do his ideas and behavior make any sense to you at all?

5. Read carefully the last paragraph of the story. In terms of what happened in the story, explain what the bishop must have meant in each sentence of that paragraph.

6. In real life, very few policemen or judges would think of treating a man with a record like Valjean's as the bishop treated him. What arguments would they offer for treating him more severely?

What answers would the bishop offer to these arguments?

7. Can you think of any instances in which an attitude like the bishop's toward someone who had done something wrong might have worked better than punishment and revenge?

8. Taking into account all of the preceding questions and answers on "theme," how would you express the underlying message of this story?

VOCABULARY GROWTH

Appreciating the Author's Choice of Words

In that stirring part of the story when Jean Valjean wakes in the night and stops at the bishop's bed on his way to get the silver, *light* plays an important part. The author is careful to describe the *light effects* as Jean Valjean moves, and stops, and moves again. Valjean starts in a *glimmer* among alternations (changes) of *eclipses* and *illuminations;* the glimmer resembles the *livid* light which falls through dungeon windows. When he sees the bishop, the light is described very differently. The bishop's countenance is lit up with a *radiance;* the light is described as a *luminous transparency;* the sleeping bishop appears as if in a *halo.*

1. In your dictionary, look up the meanings of each of the first four italicized words that describe the light that surrounded Jean Valjean. What is the total impression you get of the kind of world he seemed to be moving in?

2. Now look up the meanings of each of the last four italicized words that describe the light that surrounded the bishop. Do you see the contrast? How does this contrast help to bring out the theme of the story?

3. Consider this passage from page 74 again:
    "A reflection from this heaven shone upon the bishop. "

"But it was also a *luminous transparency,* for this heaven was within him. . . ."

What do the meanings of *luminous* and *transparency* tell about the bishop's character?

4. Sometime you may be writing a story or an essay in which you want to express different shades of meaning centering around one idea, as Victor Hugo did here with the idea of light. A good source of words that express such shades of meaning is *Roget's Thesaurus,* which offers a variety of words to express almost any idea you can think of. Under *light* for example, you find such words as *ray, beam, gleam, streak, glare, glow, glimmer,* and many, many others.

Make the acquaintance of this excellent reference book and use it.

FOR COMPOSITION

1. You can probably think of an occasion when someone in authority—a parent, a teacher, a policeman—was too severe with someone, possibly yourself; perhaps a more kindly approach would have accomplished more. Write a short composition in which you tell what happened and explain why a more kindly approach would have gotten better results.

2. Do you think the bishop had any permanent influence on Jean Valjean? If you think he did, write a paragraph in which you explain how Jean Valjean must have changed after this incident. If you think the bishop had no permanent influence on Jean Valjean, write a paragraph explaining why you think so.

What Men Live By

LEO TOLSTOY

A poor Russian shoemaker meets a helpless,
mysterious stranger on a freezing-cold night, with
most unexpected results. Here is a story by one
of the greatest writers the world has ever known.

A SHOEMAKER named Simon, who had neither
house nor land of his own, lived with his wife and children
in a peasant's hut and earned his living by his work. Work
was cheap but bread was dear, and what he earned he spent
for food. The man and his wife had but one sheep-skin coat
between them for winter wear, and even that was worn to
tatters, and this was the second year he had been wanting
to buy sheep-skins for a new coat. Before winter Simon saved
up a little money: a three-rúble note lay hidden in his wife's
box, and five rúbles and twenty kopéks were owed him by
customers in the village.

So one morning he prepared to go to the village to buy

86 the sheep-skins. He put on over his shirt his wife's wadded nankeen jacket, and over that he put his own cloth coat. He took the three-rúble note in his pocket, cut himself a stick to serve as a staff, and started off after breakfast. "I'll collect the five rúbles that are due to me," thought he, "add the three I have got, and that will be enough to buy sheep-skins for the winter coat."

He came to the village and called at a peasant's hut, but the man was not at home. The peasant's wife promised that the money should be paid next week, but she would not pay it herself. Then Simon called on another peasant, but this one swore he had no money, and would only pay twenty kopéks which he owed for a pair of boots Simon had mended. Simon then tried to buy the sheep-skins on credit but the dealer would not trust him.

"Bring your money," said he, "then you may have your pick of the skins. We know what debt-collecting is like."

So all the business the shoemaker did was to get the twenty kopéks for boots he had mended, and to take a pair of felt boots a peasant gave him to sole with leather.

Simon felt downhearted. He spent the twenty kopéks on vódka, and started homewards without having bought any skins. In the morning he had felt the frost; but now, after drinking the vódka, he felt warm even without a sheep-skin coat. He trudged along, striking his stick on the frozen earth with one hand, swinging the felt boots with the other, and talking to himself.

"I'm quite warm," said he, "though I have no sheep-skin coat. I've had a drop and it runs through all my veins. I need no sheep-skins. I go along and don't worry about anything. That's the sort of man I am! What do I care? I can live without sheep-skins. I don't need them. My wife will fret, to be sure. And, true enough, it *is* a shame; one works all day long and then does not get paid. Stop a bit! If you don't bring that money along, sure enough I'll skin you, blessed if I don't. How's that? He pays twenty kopéks at a time! What can I do with twenty kopéks? Drink it—that's all one can do! Hard up, he says he is! So he may be—but what about me? You have house, and cattle, and everything; I've only what I stand up in! You have corn of your own growing, I have to buy every grain. Do what I will, I must spend three rúbles every week for bread alone. I come home and find the bread all used up and I have to fork out another rúble and a half. So just you pay up what you owe, and no nonsense about it!"

By this time he had nearly reached the shrine at the bend of the road. Looking up, he saw something whitish behind the shrine. The daylight was fading, and the shoemaker peered at the thing without being able to make out what it was. "There was no white stone here before. Can it be an ox? It's not like an ox. It has a head like a man, but it's too white; and what could a man be doing there?"

He came closer, so that it was clearly visible. To his surprise it really was a man, alive or dead, sitting naked, leaning motionless against the shrine. Terror seized the shoemaker, and he thought, "Someone has killed him, stripped him, and left him here. If I meddle I shall surely get into trouble."

So the shoemaker went on. He passed in front of the shrine so that he could not see the man. When he had gone some way he looked back, and saw that the man was no longer leaning against the shrine, but was moving as if looking towards him. The shoemaker felt more frightened than before, and thought, "Shall I go back to him or shall

I go on? If I go near him something dreadful may happen. Who knows who the fellow is? He has not come here for any good. If I go near him he may jump up and throttle me, and there will be no getting away. Or if not, he'd still be a burden on one's hands. What could I do with a naked man? I couldn't give him my last clothes. Heaven only help me to get away!"

So the shoemaker hurried on, leaving the shrine behind him—when suddenly his conscience smote him and he stopped in the road.

"What are you doing, Simon?" said he to himself. "The man may be dying of want, and you slip past afraid. Have you grown so rich as to be afraid of robbers? Ah, Simon, shame on you!"

So he turned back and went up to the man.

SIMON approached the stranger, looked at him, and saw that he was a young man, fit, with no bruises on his body, but evidently freezing and frightened, and he sat there leaning back without looking up at Simon, as if too faint to lift his eyes. Simon went close to him and then the man seemed to wake up. Turning his head, he opened his eyes and looked into Simon's face. That one look was enough to make Simon fond of the man. He threw the felt boots on the ground, undid his sash, laid it on the boots, and took off his cloth coat.

"It's not a time for talking," said he. "Come, put this coat on at once!" And Simon took the man by the elbows and helped him to rise. As he stood there, Simon saw that his body was clean and in good condition, his hands and feet shapely, and his face good and kind. He threw his coat over the man's shoulders, but the latter could not find the sleeves.

Simon guided his arms into them, and drawing the coat well on, wrapped it closely about him, tying the sash around the man's waist.

Simon even took off his torn cap to put it on the man's head, but then his own head felt cold and he thought: "I'm quite bald, while he has long curly hair." So he put his cap on his own head again. "It will be better to give him something for his feet," thought he; and he made the man sit down and helped him to put on the felt boots, saying, "There, friend, now move about and warm yourself. Other matters can be settled later on. Can you walk?"

The man stood up and looked kindly at Simon, but could not say a word.

"Why don't you speak?" said Simon. "It's too cold to stay here, we must be getting home. There now, take my stick, and if you're feeling weak lean on that. Now step out!"

The man started walking and moved easily, not lagging behind.

As they went along, Simon asked him, "And where do you belong to?"

"I'm not from these parts."

"I thought as much. I know the folks hereabouts. But how did you come to be there by the shrine?"

"I cannot tell."

"Has some one been ill-treating you?"

"No one has ill-treated me. God has punished me."

"Of course God rules all. Still, you'll have to find food and shelter somewhere. Where do you want to go to?"

"It is all the same to me."

Simon was amazed. The man did not look like a rogue, and he spoke gently, but yet he gave no account of himself. Still Simon thought, "Who knows what may have happened?" And he said to the stranger: "Well then, come home with me and at least warm yourself awhile."

So Simon walked towards his home, and the stranger kept up with him, walking at his side. The wind had risen and Simon felt it cold under his shirt. He was getting over his tipsiness by now and began to feel the frost. He went along sniffling and wrapping his wife's jacket round him, and he thought to himself: "There now—talk about sheep-skins! I went out for sheep-skins and come home without even a coat to my back, and what is more, I'm bringing a naked man along with me. Matrëna won't be pleased!" And when he thought of his wife he felt sad; but when he looked at the stranger and remembered how he had looked up at him at the shrine, his heart was glad.

SIMON's wife had everything ready early that day. She had cut wood, brought water, fed the children, eaten her own meal, and now she sat thinking. She wondered when she ought to make bread: now or to-morrow? There was still a large piece left.

"If Simon has had some dinner in town," thought she, "and does not eat much for supper, the bread will last out another day."

She weighed the piece of bread in her hand again and again, and thought: "I won't make any more to-day. We have only enough flour left to bake one batch. We can manage to make this last out till Friday."

So Matrëna put away the bread, and sat down at the table to patch her husband's shirt. While she worked she thought how her husband was buying skins for a winter coat.

"If only the dealer does not cheat him. My good man is much too simple; he cheats nobody, but any child can take him in. Eight rúbles is a lot of money—he should get a good coat at that price. Not tanned skins, but still a proper winter coat. How difficult it was last winter to get on without a warm coat. I could neither get down to the river nor go out anywhere. When he went out he put on all we had, and there was nothing left for me. He did not start very early to-day, but still it's time he was back. I only hope he has not gone on the spree!"

Hardly had Matrëna thought this than steps were heard on the threshold and some one entered. Matrëna stuck her needle into her work and went out into the passage. There she saw two men: Simon, and with him a man without a hat and wearing felt boots.

Matrëna noticed at once that her husband smelt of spirits. "There now, he has been drinking," thought she. And when she saw that he was coatless, had only her jacket on, brought no parcel, stood there silent, and seemed ashamed, her heart was ready to break with disappointment. "He has drunk the money," thought she, "and has been on the spree with some good-for-nothing fellow whom he has brought home with him."

Matrëna let them pass into the hut, followed them in, and saw that the stranger was a young, slight man, wearing her husband's coat. There was no shirt to be seen under it, and he had no hat. Having entered, he stood neither moving nor raising his eyes, and Matrëna thought: "He must be a bad man—he's afraid."

Matrëna frowned, and stood beside the stove looking to see what they would do.

Simon took off his cap and sat down on the bench as if things were all right.

"Come, Matrëna; if supper is ready, let us have some."

Matrëna muttered something to herself and did not move, but stayed where she was, by the stove. She looked first at the one and then at the other of them and only shook her head. Simon saw that his wife was annoyed, but tried to pass it off. Pretending not to notice anything, he took the stranger by the arm.

"Sit down, friend," said he, "and let us have some supper."

The stranger sat down on the bench.

"Haven't you cooked anything for us?" said Simon.

Matrëna's anger boiled over. "I've cooked, but not for you. It seems to me you have drunk your wits away. You went to buy a sheep-skin coat, but come home without so much as the coat you had on, and bring a naked vagabond home with you. I have no supper for drunkards like you."

"That's enough, Matrëna. Don't wag your tongue without reason! You had better ask what sort of man——"

"And you tell me what you've done with the money?"

Simon found the pocket of the jacket, drew out the three-rúble note, and unfolded it.

"Here is the money. Trífonov did not pay, but promises to pay soon."

Matrëna got still more angry; he had bought no sheep-skins, but had put his only coat on some naked fellow and had even brought him to their house.

She snatched up the note from the table, took it to put away in safety, and said: "I have no supper for you. We can't feed all the naked drunkards in the world."

"There now, Matrëna, hold your tongue a bit. First hear what a man has to say——!"

"Much wisdom I shall hear from a drunken fool. I was right in not wanting to marry you—a drunkard. The linen my mother gave me you drank; and now you've been to buy a coat—and have drunk it too!"

Simon tried to explain to his wife that he had only spent

twenty kopéks; tried to tell how he had found the man—but
Matrëna would not let him get a word in. She talked nineteen
to the dozen, and dragged in things that had happened ten
years before.

Matrëna talked and talked, and at last she flew at Simon
and seized him by the sleeve.

"Give me my jacket. It is the only one I have, and you
must needs take it from me and wear it yourself. Give it here,
you mangy dog, and may the devil take you."

Simon began to pull off the jacket, and turned a sleeve of
it inside out; Matrëna seized the jacket and it burst its seams.
She snatched it up, threw it over her head and went to the
door. She meant to go out, but stopped undecided—she
wanted to work off her anger, but she also wanted to learn
what sort of a man the stranger was.

MATRËNA stopped and said: "If he were a good man he
would not be naked. Why, he hasn't even a shirt on him. If
he were all right, you would say where you came across
the fellow."

"That's just what I am trying to tell you," said Simon. "As
I came to the shrine I saw him sitting all naked and frozen.
It isn't quite the weather to sit about naked! God sent me to
him or he would have perished. What was I to do? How
do we know what may have happened to him? Don't be
so angry, Matrëna. It is a sin. Remember, we must all
die one day."

Angry words rose to Matrëna's lips, but she looked at the
stranger and was silent. He sat on the edge of the bench,
motionless, his hands folded on his knees, his head drooping
on his breast, his eyes closed, and his brows knit as if in pain.
Matrëna was silent, and Simon said: "Matrëna, have you no
love of God?"

Matrëna heard these words, and as she looked at the stranger, suddenly her heart softened towards him. She came back from the door, and going to the stove she got out the supper. Setting a cup on the table, she poured out some *kvas*. Then she brought out the last piece of bread and set out a knife and spoons.

"Eat, if you want to," said she.

Simon drew the stranger to the table.

"Take your place, young man," said he.

Simon cut the bread, crumbled it into the broth, and they began to eat. Matrëna sat at the corner of the table, resting her head on her hand and looking at the stranger.

And Matrëna was touched with pity for the stranger and began to feel fond of him. And at once the stranger's face lit up; his brows were no longer bent, he raised his eyes and smiled at Matrëna.

When they had finished supper, the woman cleared away the things and began questioning the stranger. "Where are you from?" said she.

"I am not from these parts."

"But how did you come to be on the road?"

"I may not tell."

"Did someone rob you?"

"God punished me."

"And you were lying there naked?"

"Yes, naked and freezing. Simon saw me and had pity on me. He took off his coat, put it on me, and brought me here. And you have fed me, given me drink, and shown pity on me. God will reward you!"

Matrëna rose, took from the window Simon's old shirt she had been patching, and gave it to the stranger. She also brought out a pair of trousers for him.

"There," said she, "I see you have no shirt. Put this on, **95** and lie down where you please, in the loft or on the stove."

The stranger took off the coat, put on the shirt, and lay down in the loft. Matrëna put out the candle, took the coat, and climbed to where her husband lay on the stove.

Matrëna drew the skirts of the coat over her and lay down but could not sleep; she could not get the stranger out of her mind.

When she remembered that he had eaten their last piece of bread and that there was none for to-morrow, and thought of the shirt and trousers she had given away, she felt grieved; but when she remembered how he had smiled, her heart was glad.

Long did Matrëna lie awake, and she noticed that Simon also was awake—he drew the coat towards him.

"Simon!"

"Well?"

"You have had the last of the bread and I have not put any to rise. I don't know what we shall do to-morrow. Perhaps I can borrow some of neighbor Martha."

"If we're alive we shall find something to eat."

The woman lay still awhile, and then said, "He seems a good man, but why does he not tell us who he is?"

"I suppose he has his reasons."

"Simon!"

"Well?"

"We give; but why does nobody give us anything?"

Simon did not know what to say; so he only said, "Let us stop talking," and turned over and went to sleep.

In the morning Simon awoke. The children were still asleep; his wife had gone to the neighbor's to borrow some bread. The stranger alone was sitting on the bench, dressed in the old shirt and trousers, and looking upwards. His face was brighter than it had been the day before.

Simon said to him, "Well, friend; the belly wants bread and the naked body clothes. One has to work for a living. What work do you know?"

"I do not know any."

This surprised Simon, but he said, "Men who want to learn can learn anything."

"Men work and I will work also."

"What is your name?"

"Michael."

"Well, Michael, if you don't wish to talk about yourself, that is your own affair; but you'll have to earn a living for yourself. If you will work as I tell you, I will give you food and shelter."

"May God reward you! I will learn. Show me what to do."

Simon took yarn, put it round his thumb and began to twist it.

"It is easy enough—see!"

Michael watched him, put some yarn round his own thumb in the same way, caught the knack, and twisted the yarn also.

Then Simon showed him how to wax the thread. This also Michael mastered. Next Simon showed him how to twist the bristle in, and how to sew, and this, too, Michael learned at once.

Whatever Simon showed him he understood at once, and after three days he worked as if he had sewn boots all his life. He worked without stopping and ate little. When work was over he sat silently, looking upwards. He hardly went into the street, spoke only when necessary, and neither joked nor laughed. They never saw him smile, except that first evening when Matrëna gave them supper.

DAY by day and week by week the year went round. Michael lived and worked with Simon. His fame spread till people said that no one sewed boots so neatly and strongly as Simon's workman, Michael; from all the district round people came to Simon for their boots, and he began to be well off.

One winter day, as Simon and Michael sat working, a carriage on sledge-runners, with three horses and with bells, drove up to the hut. They looked out of the window; the carriage stopped at their door, a fine servant jumped down from the box and opened the door. A gentleman in a fur coat got out and walked up to Simon's hut. Up jumped Matrëna and opened the door wide. The gentleman stooped to enter the hut, and when he drew himself up again his head nearly reached the ceiling and he seemed quite to fill his end of the room.

Simon rose, bowed, and looked at the gentleman with astonishment. He had never seen anyone like him. Simon himself was lean, Michael was thin, and Matrëna was dry as a bone, but this man was like someone from another world: red-faced, burly, with a neck like a bull's, and looking altogether as if he were cast in iron.

The gentleman puffed, threw off his fur coat, sat down on the bench, and said, "Which of you is the master bootmaker?"

"I am, your Excellency," said Simon, coming forward.

Then the gentleman shouted to his lad, "Hey Fédka, bring the leather!"

The servant ran in, bringing a parcel. The gentleman took the parcel and put it on the table.

"Untie it," said he. The lad untied it.

The gentleman pointed to the leather.

"Look here, shoemaker," said he, "do you see this leather?"

"Yes, your Honor."

"But do you know what sort of leather it is?"

Simon felt the leather and said, "It is good leather."

"Good, indeed! Why, you fool, you never saw such leather before in your life. It's German, and cost twenty rúbles."

Simon was frightened, and said, "Where should I ever see leather like that?"

"Just so! Now, can you make it into boots for me?"

"Yes, your Excellency, I can."

Then the gentleman shouted at him: "You *can*, can you? Well, remember whom you are to make them for, and what the leather is. You must make me boots that will wear for a year, neither losing shape nor coming unsewn. If you can do it, take the leather and cut it up; but if you can't, say so. I warn you now, if your boots come unsewn or lose shape within a year I will have you put in prison. If they don't burst or lose shape for a year, I will pay you ten rúbles for your work."

Simon was frightened and did not know what to say. He glanced at Michael and, nudging him with his elbow, whispered: "Shall I take the work?"

Michael nodded his head as if to say, "Yes, take it."

Simon did as Michael advised and undertook to make boots that would not lose shape or split for a whole year.

Calling his servant, the gentleman told him to pull the boot off his left leg, which he stretched out.

"Take my measure!" said he.

Simon stitched a paper measure seventeen inches long, smoothed it out, knelt down, wiped his hands well on his apron so as not to soil the gentleman's sock, and began to measure. He measured the sole, and round the instep, and began to measure the calf of the leg, but the paper was too short. The calf of the leg was as thick as a beam.

"Mind you don't make it too tight in the leg."

Simon stitched on another strip of paper. The gentleman twitched his toes about in his sock looking round at those in the hut, and as he did so he noticed Michael.

"Whom have you there?" asked he.

"That is my workman. He will sew the boots."

"Mind," said the gentleman to Michael, "remember to make them so that they will last me a year."

Simon also looked at Michael, and saw that Michael was not looking at the gentleman, but was gazing into the corner behind the gentleman, as if he saw some one there. Michael looked and looked, and suddenly he smiled, and his face became brighter.

"What are you grinning at, you fool?" thundered the gentleman. "You had better look to it that the boots are ready in time."

"They shall be ready in good time," said Michael.

"Mind it is so," said the gentleman, and he put on his boots and his fur coat, wrapped the latter round him, and went to the door. But he forgot to stoop, and struck his head against the lintel.

He swore and rubbed his head. Then he took his seat in the carriage and drove away.

When he had gone, Simon said: "There's a figure of a man for you! You could not kill him with a mallet. He almost knocked out the lintel, but little harm it did him."

And Matrëna said: "Living as he does, how should he not grow strong? Death itself can't touch such a rock as that."

THEN Simon said to Michael: "Well, we have taken the work, but we must see we don't get into trouble over it. The leather is dear, and the gentleman hot-tempered. We must make no mistakes. Come, your eye is truer and your hands have become nimbler than mine, so you take this measure and cut out the boots. I will finish off the sewing of the vamps."

Michael did as he was told. He took the leather, spread it out on the table, folded it in two, took a knife and began to cut out.

Matrëna came and watched him cutting, and was surprised to see how he was doing it. Matrëna was accustomed to seeing boots made, and she looked and saw that Michael was not cutting the leather for boots, but was cutting it round.

She wished to say something, but she thought to herself: "Perhaps I do not understand how gentlemen's boots should be made. I suppose Michael knows more about it—and I won't interfere."

When Michael had cut up the leather he took a thread and began to sew not with two ends, as boots are sewn, but with a single end, as for soft slippers.

Again Matrëna wondered, but again she did not interfere. Michael sewed on steadily till noon. Then Simon rose for dinner, looked around, and saw that Michael had made slippers out of the gentleman's leather.

"Ah!" groaned Simon, and he thought, "How is it that Michael, who has been with me a whole year and never made a mistake before, should do such a dreadful thing? The gentleman ordered high boots, welted, with whole fronts, and Michael has made soft slippers with single soles, and has wasted the leather. What am I to say to the gentleman? I can never replace leather such as this."

And he said to Michael, "What are you doing, friend? You have ruined me! You know the gentleman ordered high boots, but see what you have made!"

Hardly had he begun to rebuke Michael when "rat-tat" went the iron ring that hung at the door. Some one was knocking. They looked out of the window; a man had come on horseback and was fastening his horse. They opened the door, and the servant who had been with the gentleman came in.

"Good day," said he.

"Good day," replied Simon. "What can we do for you?"

"My mistress has sent me about the boots."

"What about the boots?"

"Why, my master no longer needs them. He is dead."

"Is it possible?"

"He did not live to get home after leaving you, but died in the carriage. When we reached home and the servants came to help him alight, he rolled over like a sack. He was dead already, and so stiff that he could hardly be got out of the carriage. My mistress sent me here, saying: 'Tell the bootmaker that the gentleman who ordered boots of him and left the leather for them no longer needs the boots, but that he must quickly make soft slippers for the corpse. Wait till they are ready and bring them back with you.' That is why I have come."

Michael gathered up the remnants of the leather; rolled them up, took the soft slippers he had made, slapped them together, wiped them down with his apron, and handed them and the roll of leather to the servant, who took them and said: "Good-bye, masters, and good day to you!"

ANOTHER year passed, and another, and Michael was now living his sixth year with Simon. He lived as before. He went nowhere, only spoke when necessary, and had only smiled twice in all those years—once when Matrëna gave him food, and a second time when the gentleman was in their hut. Simon was more than pleased with his workman. He never now asked him where he came from, and only feared lest Michael should go away.

They were all at home one day. Matrëna was putting iron pots in the oven; the children were running along the benches and looking out of the window; Simon was sewing at one window and Michael was fastening on a heel at the other.

One of the boys ran along the bench to Michael, leant on his shoulder, and looked out of the window.

"Look, Uncle Michael! There is a lady with little girls! She seems to be coming here. And one of the girls is lame."

When the boy said that, Michael dropped his work, turned to the window, and looked out into the street.

Simon was surprised. Michael never used to look out into the street, but now he pressed against the window, staring at something. Simon also looked out and saw that a well-dressed woman was really coming to his hut, leading by the hand two little girls in fur coats and woolen shawls. The girls could hardly be told one from the other, except that one of them was crippled in her left leg and walked with a limp.

The woman stepped into the porch and entered the passage. Feeling about for the entrance she found the latch, which she lifted and opened the door. She let the two girls go in first, and followed them into the hut.

"Good day, good folk!"

"Pray come in," said Simon. "What can we do for you?"

The woman sat down by the table. The two little girls pressed close to her knees, afraid of the people in the hut.

"I want leather shoes made for these two little girls, for spring."

"We can do that. We never have made such small shoes, but we can make them; either welted or turnover shoes, linen-lined. My man, Michael, is a master at the work."

Simon glanced at Michael and saw that he had left his work and was sitting with his eyes fixed on the little girls. Simon was surprised. It was true the girls were pretty, with black eyes, plump, and rosy-cheeked, and they wore nice kerchiefs and fur coats, but still Simon could not understand why Michael should look at them like that—just as if he had known them before. He was puzzled, but went on talking with the woman and arranging the price. Having fixed it, he prepared the measure. The woman lifted the lame girl on her lap and said: "Take two measures from this little girl. Make one shoe for the lame foot and three for the sound one. They both have the same-sized feet. They are twins."

Simon took the measure and, speaking of the lame girl, said: "How did it happen to her? She is such a pretty girl. Was she born so?"

"No, her mother crushed her leg."

Then Matrëna joined in. She wondered who this woman was and whose the children were, so she said: "Are not you their mother, then?"

"No, my good woman; I am neither their mother nor any

104 relation to them. They were quite strangers to me, but I adopted them."

"They are not your children and yet you are so fond of them?"

"How can I help being fond of them? I fed them both at my own breasts. I had a child of my own, but God took him. I was not so fond of him as I now am of these."

"Then whose children are they?"

THE woman, having begun talking, told them the whole story.

"It is about six years since their parents died, both in one week: their father was buried on the Tuesday, and their mother died on the Friday. These orphans were born three days after their father's death, and their mother did not live another day. My husband and I were then living as peasants in the village. We were neighbors of theirs, our yard being next to theirs. Their father was a lonely man, a wood-cutter in the forest. When felling trees one day they let one fall on him. It fell across his body and crushed his bowels out. They hardly got him home before his soul went to God; and that same week his wife gave birth to twins—these little girls. She was poor and alone; she had no one, young or old, with her. Alone she gave them birth, and alone she met her death.

"The next morning I went to see her, but when I entered the hut, she, poor thing, was already stark and cold. In dying she had rolled on to this child and crushed her leg. The village folk came to the hut, washed her body, laid her out, made a coffin, and buried her. They were good folk. The babies were left alone. What was to be done with them? I was the only woman there who had a baby at the time. I was nursing my first-born—eight weeks old. So I took them for a time. The peasants came together, and thought and thought what to do with them; and at last they said to me: 'For the present, Mary, you had better keep the girls, and later on we will arrange what to do for them.' So I nursed the sound one at my breast, but at first I did not feed this crippled one. I did not suppose she would live. But then I thought to myself, why should the poor innocent suffer? I pitied her and began to feed her. And so I fed my own boy and these two—the three of them—at my own breast. I was young and strong and had good food, and God gave me so much milk that at times it even overflowed. I used sometimes to feed two at a time, while the third was waiting. When one had had enough I nursed the third. And God so ordered it that these grew up, while my own was buried before he was two years old. And I had no more children, though we prospered. Now my husband is working for the corn merchant at the mill. The pay is good and we are well off. But I have no children of my own, and how lonely I should be without these little girls! How can I help loving them! They are the joy of my life!"

She pressed the lame little girl to her with her one hand, while with the other she wiped the tears from her cheeks.

And Matrëna sighed, and said: "The proverb is true that says, 'One may live without father or mother, but one cannot live without God.'"

So they talked together, when suddenly the whole hut was lighted up as though by summer lightning from the corner where Michael sat. They all looked towards him and saw him sitting, his hands folded on his knees, gazing upwards and smiling.

THE woman went away with the girls. Michael rose from the bench, put down his work, and took off his apron. Then, bowing low to Simon and his wife, he said: "Farewell, mas-

106 ters. God has forgiven me. I ask your forgiveness, too, for anything done amiss."

And they saw that a light shone from Michael. And Simon rose, bowed down to Michael, and said: "I see, Michael, that you are no common man, and I can neither keep you nor question you. Only tell me this: how is it that when I found you and brought you home, you were gloomy, and when my wife gave you food you smiled at her and became brighter? Then when the gentleman came to order the boots, you smiled again and became brighter still? And now, when this woman brought the little girls, you smiled a third time and have become as bright as day? Tell me, Michael, why does your face shine so, and why did you smile those three times?"

And Michael answered: "Light shines from me because I have been punished, but now God has pardoned me. And I smiled three times, because God sent me to learn three truths, and I have learnt them. One I learnt when your wife pitied me, and that is why I smiled the first time. The second I learnt when the rich man ordered the boots, and then I smiled again. And now, when I saw those little girls, I learnt the third and last truth, and I smiled the third time."

And Simon said, "Tell me, Michael, what did God punish you for? And what were the three truths—that I, too, may know them?"

And Michael answered: "God punished me for disobeying Him. I was an angel in heaven and disobeyed God. God sent me to fetch a woman's soul. I flew to earth, and saw a sick woman lying alone who had just given birth to twin girls. They moved feebly at their mother's side but she could not lift them to her breast. When she saw me, she understood that God had sent me for her soul, and she wept and

said: 'Angel of God! My husband has just been buried, killed
by a falling tree. I have neither sister, nor aunt, nor mother:
no one to care for my orphans. Do not take my soul! Let me
nurse my babes, feed them, and set them on their feet before
I die. Children cannot live without father or mother.' And
I hearkened to her. I placed one child at her breast and gave
the other into her arms, and returned to the Lord in heaven.
I flew to the Lord, and said: 'I could not take the soul of the
mother. Her husband was killed by a tree; the woman has
twins and prays that her soul may not be taken. She says:
"Let me nurse and feed my children, and set them on their
feet. Children cannot live without father or mother." I have
not taken her soul.' And God said: 'Go—take the mother's
soul, and learn three truths: Learn *What dwells in man*,
What is not given to man, and *What men live by*. When thou
hast learnt these things, thou shalt return to heaven.' So I
flew again to earth and took the mother's soul. The babes
dropped from her breasts. Her body rolled over on the bed
and crushed one babe, twisting its leg. I rose above the
village, wishing to take her soul to God, but a wind seized
me and my wings drooped and dropped off. Her soul rose
alone to God, while I fell to earth by the roadside."

AND Simon and Matrëna understood who it was that had
lived with them, and whom they had clothed and fed. And
they wept with awe and with joy. And the angel said: "I
was alone in the field, naked. I had never known human
needs, cold and hunger, till I became a man. I was famished,
frozen, and did not know what to do. I saw, near the field
I was in, a shrine built for God, and I went to it hoping to
find shelter. But the shrine was locked and I could not enter.
So I sat down behind the shrine to shelter myself at least

from the wind. Evening drew on, I was hungry, frozen, and in pain. Suddenly I heard a man coming along the road. He carried a pair of boots and was talking to himself. For the first time since I became a man I saw the mortal face of a man, and his face seemed terrible to me and I turned from it. And I heard the man talking to himself of how to cover his body from the cold in winter, and how to feed wife and children. And I thought: 'I am perishing of cold and hunger and here is a man thinking only of how to clothe himself and his wife, and how to get bread for themselves. He cannot help me.' When the man saw me he frowned and became still more terrible, and passed me by on the other side. I despaired; but suddenly I heard him coming back. I looked up and did not recognize the same man: before, I had seen death in his face; but now he was alive and I recognized in him the presence of God. He came up to me, clothed me, took me with him, and brought me to his home. I entered the house; a woman came to meet us and began to speak. The woman was still more terrible than the man had been; the spirit of death came from her mouth; I could not breathe for the stench of death that spread around her. She wished to drive me out into the cold, and I knew that if she did so she would die. Suddenly her husband spoke to her of God, and the woman changed at once. And when she brought me food and looked at me, I glanced at her and saw that death no longer dwelt in her; she had become alive, and in her too I saw God.

"Then I remembered the first lesson God had set me: '*Learn what dwells in man.*' And I understood that in man dwells Love! I was glad that God had already begun to show me what He had promised, and I smiled for the first time. But I had not yet learnt all. I did not yet know *What is not given to man,* and *What men live by.*

"I lived with you and a year passed. A man came to order boots that should wear for a year without losing shape or cracking. I looked at him, and suddenly, behind his shoulder, I saw my comrade—the angel of death. None but me saw that angel; but I knew him, and knew that before the sun set he would take that rich man's soul. And I thought to myself, 'The man is making preparations for a year and does not know that he will die before evening.' And I remembered God's second saying, '*Learn what is not given to man.*'

"What dwells in man I already knew. Now I learnt what is not given him. It is not given to man to know his own needs. And I smiled for the second time. I was glad to have seen my comrade angel—glad also that God had revealed to me the second saying.

"But I still did not know all. I did not know *What men live by*. And I lived on, waiting till God should reveal to me the last lesson. In the sixth year came the girl-twins with the woman; and I recognized the girls and heard how they had been kept alive. Having heard the story, I thought, 'Their mother besought me for the children's sake, and I believed her when she said that children cannot live without father or mother; but a stranger has nursed them, and has brought them up.' And when the woman showed her love for the children that were not her own, and wept over them, I saw in her the living God, and understood *What men live by*. And I knew that God had revealed to me the last lesson, and had forgiven my sin. And then I smiled for the third time."

AND the angel's body was bared, and he was clothed in light so that eye could not look on him; and his voice grew louder, as though it came not from him but from heaven above. And the angel said:

"I have learnt that all men live not by care for themselves, but by love.

"It was not given to the mother to know what her children needed for their life. Nor was it given to the rich man to know what he himself needed. Nor is it given to any man to know whether, when evening comes, he will need boots for his body or slippers for his corpse.

"I remained alive when I was a man, not by care of myself but because love was present in a passer-by, and because he and his wife pitied and loved me. The orphans remained alive not because of their mother's care, but because there was love in the heart of a woman, a stranger to them, who pitied and loved them. And all men live not by the thought they spend on their own welfare, but because love exists in man.

"I knew before that God gave life to men and desires that they should live; now I understood more than that.

"I understood that God does not wish men to live apart, and therefore he does not reveal to them what each one needs for himself; but he wishes them to live united, and therefore reveals to each of them what is necessary for all.

"I have now understood that though it seems to men that they live by care for themselves, in truth it is love alone by which they live. He who has love, is in God, and God is in him, for God is love."

And the angel sang praise to God, so that the hut trembled at his voice. The roof opened, and a column of fire rose from earth to heaven. Simon and his wife and children fell to the ground. Wings appeared upon the angel's shoulders and he rose into the heavens.

And when Simon came to himself the hut stood as before, and there was no one in it but his own family.

About the Author

Leo Tolstoy was born in 1828, the child of typical Russian aristocrats. While at the university, he was influenced by some of the revolutionary writers of France to give up his studies and turn to the "more natural" life of farming. Later he drifted back to aristocratic living, but eventually he grew more and more to dislike the life of the rich. He decided to dedicate his life to helping the poor peasants in Russia. In the meantime he had written many short stories and novels. His most famous novel, *War and Peace,* is a classic story of Russian life during the war with Napoleon.

Tolstoy also became interested in religion, especially in the religious ideas of love and brotherhood which appear in "What Men Live By." He believed that the rich had been corrupted by wealth. To carry out his ideas, Tolstoy personally gave up his wealth and dressed and worked like a peasant.

FOR DISCUSSION

This is a story in which the author wanted to convey some truth about human life. The angel Michael finally explains this truth. If you look back at the story you will discover that, as in the case of "The Bishop's Silver," the theme arose out of the interaction of the characters, and out of the events that occurred (the plot).

It is important first to examine the characters.

Understanding the Characters

1. Neither Simon nor Matrëna was a perfect character. What faults did you find in them?

Suppose they *had* been perfect characters. Would the story have been a better one or a worse one? Why?

2. Matrëna says of the gentleman who came to have shoes made: " 'Death itself can't touch such a rock as that.' " What was there about his appearance and behavior that gave her such an impression?

Were you impressed by him in the same way as Matrëna was? Explain your own feelings about him.

A turn of events in which the opposite of what had been expected happens is called *irony*. What ironical thing happened to the gentleman?

3. What was there about the details of the life of the woman who came with the children that made her especially remarkable?

4. Michael is puzzling and mystifying for most of the story. List the things that puzzle or mystify, and then indicate how each of them is cleared up at the end of the story.

Understanding the Theme

1. Together the three truths of Michael make up the theme of the story. What are these truths?

2. Which of these truths were developed by the interaction of Simon, Matrëna, and Michael?

3. Which truth, or truths, were developed and illustrated in the interaction of the "gentleman" and Simon and Michael? See if you can find more than one truth in this part of the story.

4. Which truth, or truths, were developed in the interaction of the woman and Michael?

5. The question which the title, "What Men Live By," seems to ask is answered in Michael's sentence: " 'I have now understood that though it seems to men that they live by care for themselves, in truth it is love alone by which they live.' "

   a. What does that sentence really mean? Explain both parts of it.

b. In the light of this sentence, one character in the story could not have been *truly living*. Who? Why?

c. What people do you know who are not truly *living* in the sense that Michael used the word?

d. What people do you know, either alive today or from the past, who *lived* in Michael's sense of the word?

VOCABULARY GROWTH

Using Context to Unlock Word Meanings

The most natural way in which a good vocabulary is built is through wide reading. If you read a great deal and have an interest in new words, many of them will become part of your vocabulary without the need to go to a dictionary.

The trick is to observe the context of a word—its surroundings, the words that accompany it, the kind of situation in which it occurs.

On page 99, for example, the "gentleman" is leaving Simon's hut. He goes to the door. "But he forgot to stoop, and struck his head against the *lintel*."

You don't have to look up *lintel* in a dictionary to understand that it must be a part of the structure just above the door.

Each of the following sentences contains an italicized word worth knowing, the meaning of which you should be able to get from the context. Check your guess with the dictionary meaning to see how close you got.

1. (Simon has just found Michael naked on the road. Michael has said that God had punished him.)
"Simon was amazed. The man did not look like a *rogue*, and he spoke gently, but yet he gave no account of himself."

2. (Simon says this to Michael.)
" 'The leather is dear, and the gentleman hot-tempered. We must make no mistakes. Come, your eye is truer

and your hands have become *nimbler* than mine, so you . . . cut out the boots.' "

3. (Michael says this to Simon and Matréna.)
" 'I was famished, frozen. . . . I saw, near the field I was in, a *shrine* built for God, and I went to it hoping to find shelter.' "

FOR COMPOSITION

1. Describe some of the changes that might take place in your community if everyone took to heart the theme of this story.

2. Some people might say of the theme, "It sounds very good, but you can't really live that way in our world." Explain in a composition why you agree or disagree with the attitude of these people.

3. "What Men Live By" is a parable, a story designed to convey a moral lesson. The Old and New Testaments of the Bible contain many parables.

Try writing a parable of your own to bring out some moral lesson. Your parable could deal with a subject such as honesty, or lying, or friendship, or selfishness, or laziness, or justice—or any other virtue or vice. Remember that you will make your point through the characters and events that you make up.

Death of a Tsotsi

ALAN PATON

This is a story about a young black boy in Johannesburg, South Africa, where the white government has passed laws that completely segregate the black people and deny them equal rights and opportunity. Spike, a member of a young black gang called the *tsotsis*, was sent to a reformatory after he was caught committing a crime. The reformatory—a rather unusual place—did something for Spike. When he got out, he wanted to quit the gang, but the gang wanted him. Who is to blame for the gangs, for the crimes, and for what happened to Spike? This story will give you much to think about.

ABRAHAM MOLETISANE was his name, but no one
ever called him anything but Spike. He was a true child of
the city, gay, careless, plausible; but for all that he was easy
to manage and anxious to please. He was clean though flashy
in his private dress. The khaki shirts and shorts of the reformatory were too drab for him, and he had a red scarf and yellow
handkerchief which he arranged to peep out of his shirt
pocket. He also had a pair of black and white shoes and a
small but highly coloured feather in his cap. Now the use of
private clothes, except after the day's work, was forbidden;
but he wore the red scarf on all occasions, saying, with an
earnest expression that changed into an enigmatic smile if
you looked too long at him, that his throat was sore. That was
a great habit of his, to look away when you talked to him, and
to smile at some unseen thing.

He passed through the first stages of the reformatory very
successfully. He had two distinct sets of visitors, one his hard-
working mother and his younger sister, and the other a group
of flashy young men from the city. His mother and the young
men never came together, and I think he arranged it so. While
we did not welcome his second set of visitors, we did not
forbid them so long as they behaved themselves; it was better
for us to know about them than otherwise.

One day his mother and sister brought a friend, Elizabeth,
who was a quiet and clean-looking person like themselves.
Spike told me that his mother wished him to marry this girl,
but that the girl was very independent, and refused to hear
of it unless he reformed and gave up the company of the
tsotsis.

"And what do you say, Spike?"

He would not look at me, but tilted his head up and surveyed the ceiling, smiling hard at it, and dropping his eyes

but not his head to take an occasional glance at me. I did not
know exactly what was in his mind, but it was clear to me
that he was beginning to feel confidence in the reformatory.

"It doesn't help to say to her, just O.K., O.K.," he said.
"She wants it done before everybody, as the Principal gives
the first freedom."
"What do you mean, before everybody?"
"Before my family and hers."
"And are you willing?"

Spike smiled harder than ever at the ceiling, as though at
some secret but delicious joy. Whether it was that he was
savouring the delight of deciding his future, I do not know.
Or whether he was savouring the delight of keeping guessing
two whole families and the reformatory, I do not know either.

He was suddenly serious. "If I promise her, I'll keep it," he
said. "But I won't be forced."
"No one's forcing you," I said.

He lowered his head and looked at me, as though I did
not understand the ways of women.

Although Spike was regarded as a weak character, he met
all the temptations of increasing physical freedom very successfully. He went to the free hostels, and after some months
there he received the special privilege of special weekend
leave to go home. He swaggered out, and he swaggered back,
punctual to the minute. How he timed it I do not know, for
he had no watch; but in all the months that he had the privilege, he was never late.

It was just after he had received his first special leave that
one of his city friends was sent to the reformatory also. The
friend's name was Walter, and within a week of his arrival he

118 and Spike had a fight, and both were sent to me. Walter
alleged that Spike had hit him first, and Spike did not deny it.

"Why did you hit him, Spike?"

"He insulted me, *meneer.*"

"How?"

At length he came out with it.

"He said I was reformed."

We could not help laughing at that, not much of course,
for it was clear to me that Spike did not understand our laughter, and that he accepted it only because he knew we were
well-disposed towards him.

*"If I said you were reformed, Spike," I said, "would you
be insulted?"*

"No, meneer."

"Then why did he insult you?"

*He thought that it was a difficult question. Then he said,
"He did not mean anything good,* meneer. *He meant I was
back to being a child."*

"You are not," I said. *"You are going forward to being a
man."*

He was mollified by that, and I warned him not to fight
again. He accepted my rebuke, but he said to me, "This fellow
is out to make trouble for me. He says I must go back to the
tsotsis when I come out."

I said to Walter, "Did you say that?"

Walter was hurt to the depths and said, "No, *meneer.*"

When they had gone I sent for de Villiers whose job it is
to know every home in Johannesburg that has a boy at the
reformatory. It was not an uncommon story, of a decent
widow left with a son and daughter. She had managed to
control the daughter, but not the son, and Spike had got in

with a gang of *tsotsis*; as a result of one of their exploits he
had found himself in court, but had not betrayed his friends.
Then he had gone to the reformatory, which apart from anything it did itself, had enabled his mother to regain her hold
on him, so that he had now decided to forsake the *tsotsis*, to
get a job through de Villiers, and to marry the girl Elizabeth
and live with her in his mother's house.

A week later Spike came to see me again.

*"The Principal must forbid these friends of Walter to visit
the reformatory,"* he said.
"Why, Spike?"
"They are planning trouble for me, meneer."

The boy was no longer smiling, but looked troubled, and
I sat considering his request. I called in de Villiers, and we
discussed it in Afrikaans, which Spike understood. But we
were talking a rather high Afrikaans for him, and his eyes
went from one face to the other, trying to follow what we
said. If I forbade these boys to visit the reformatory, what
help would that be to Spike? Would their resentment against
him be any the less? Would they forget it because they did not
see him? Might this not be a further cause for resentment
against him? After all, one cannot remake the world; one can
do all one can in a reformatory, but when the time comes,
one has to take away one's hands. It was true that de Villiers
would look after him, but such supervision had its defined
limits. As I looked at the boy's troubled face, I also was full
of trouble for him; for he had of his choice bound himself
with chains, and now, when he wanted of his choice to put
them off, he found it was not so easy to do. He looked at us
intently, and I could see that he felt excluded, and wished to
be brought in again.

"*Did you understand what we said, Spike?*"

"*Not everything,* meneer."

"*I am worried about one thing,*" I said. "*Which is better for you, to forbid these boys, or not to forbid them?*"

"*To forbid them,*" he said.

"*They might say,*" I said, "Now he'll pay for this."

"*The Principal does not understand,*" he said. "*My time is almost finished at the reformatory. I don't want trouble before I leave.*"

"*I'm not worried about trouble here,*" I said. "*I'm worried about trouble outside.*"

He looked at me anxiously, as though I had not fully grasped the matter.

"*I'm not worried about here,*" I said with asperity. "*I can look after you here. If someone tries to make trouble, do you think I can't find the truth?*"

He did not wish to doubt my ability, but he remained anxious.

"*You still want me to forbid them?*" I asked.

"*Yes,* meneer."

"*Mr. de Villiers,*" I said, "*find out all you can about these boys. Then let me know.*"

"*And then,*" I said to Spike, "*I'll talk to you about forbidding them.*"

"*They're a tough lot,*" de Villiers told me later. "*No parental control. In fact they have left home and are living with George, the head of the gang. George's mother is quite without hope for her son, but she's old now and depends on him. He gives her money, and she sees nothing, hears nothing, says nothing. She cooks for them.*"

"And they won't allow Spike to leave the gang?" I asked.

"I couldn't prove that, but it's a funny business. The reason why they don't want to let Spike go is because he has the brains and the courage. He makes the plans and they all obey him on the job. But off the job he's nobody. Off the job they all listen to George."

"Did you see George?"

"I saw George," he said, "and I reckon he's a bad fellow. He's morose and sullen, and physically bigger than Spike."

"If you got in his way," he added emphatically, "he'd wipe you out—like that."

We both sat there rather gloomy about Spike's future.

"Spike's the best of the lot," he said. "It's tragic that he ever got in with them. Now that he wants to get out . . . well . . ."

He left his sentence unfinished.

"Let's see him," I said.

"We've seen these friends of Walter's," I said to Spike, "and we don't like them very much. But whether it will help to forbid their visits, I truly do not know. But I am willing to do what you say."

"The Principal must forbid them," he said at once.

So I forbade them. They listened to me in silence, neither humble nor insolent, not affronted nor surprised; they put up no pleas or protests. George said, "Good, sir," and one by one they followed him out.

When a boy finally leaves the reformatory, he is usually elated, and does not hide his high spirits. He comes to the office for a final conversation, and goes off like one who has brought off an extraordinary coup. But Spike was subdued.

"Spike," I said privately, with only de Villiers there, "are you afraid?"

He looked down at the floor and said, "I'm not afraid," as though his fear were private also, and would neither be lessened nor made greater by confession.

He was duly married and de Villiers and I made him a present of a watch so that he could always be on time for his work. He had a good job in a factory in Industria, and worked magnificently; he saved money, and spent surprisingly little on clothes. But he had none of his old gaiety and attractive carelessness. He came home promptly, and once home, never stirred out.

It was summer when he was released, and with the approach of winter he asked if de Villiers would not see the manager of the factory, and arrange for him to leave half an hour earlier, so that he could reach his home before dark. But the manager said it was impossible, as Spike was on the kind of job that would come to a standstill if one man left earlier. De Villiers waited for him after work and he could see that the boy was profoundly depressed.

"Have they said anything to you?" de Villiers asked him.

The boy would not answer for a long time, and at last he said with a finality that was meant to stop further discussion, "They'll get me." He was devoid of hope, and did not wish to talk about it, like a man who has a great pain and does not wish to discuss it, but prefers to suffer it alone and silent. This hopelessness had affected his wife and mother and sister, so that all of them sat darkly and heavily. And de Villiers noted that there were new bars on every door and window. So he left darkly and heavily too, and Spike went with him to the little gate.

And Spike asked him, "Can I carry a knife?"

It was a hard question and the difficulty of it angered

de Villiers, so that he said harshly, "How can I say that you 123
can carry a knife?"

"You," said Spike, "my mother, my sister, Elizabeth."
He looked at de Villiers.
"I obey you all," he said, and went back into the house.

So still more darkly and heavily de Villiers went back to
the reformatory, and sitting in my office, communicated his
mood to me. We decided that he would visit Spike more often
than he visited any other boy. This he did, and he even went
to the length of calling frequently at the factory at five
o'clock, and taking Spike home. He tried to cheer and en-
courage the boy, but the dark heavy mood could not be
shifted.

One day Spike said to him, "I tell you, sir, you all did
your best for me."

The next day he was stabbed to death just by the little
gate.

In spite of my inside knowledge, Spike's death so shocked
me that I could do no work. I sat in my office, hopeless and
defeated. Then I sent for the boy Walter.

"I sent for you," I said, "to tell you that Spike is dead."

He had no answer to make. Nothing showed in his face
to tell whether he cared whether Spike were alive or dead.
He stood there impassively, obedient and respectful, ready to
go or ready to stand there for ever.

"He's dead," I said angrily. "He was killed. Don't you
care?"
"I care," he said.

124   He would have cared very deeply, had I pressed him. He surveyed me unwinkingly, ready to comply with my slightest request. Between him and me there was an unbridgeable chasm; so far as I know there was nothing in the world, not one hurt or grievance or jest or sorrow, that could have stirred us both together.

Therefore I let him go.

De Villiers and I went to the funeral, and spoke words of sympathy to Spike's mother and wife and sister. But the words fell like dead things to the ground, for something deeper than sorrow was there. We were all of us, white and black, rich and poor, learned and untutored, bowed down by a knowledge that we lived in the shadow of a great danger, and were powerless against it. It was no place for a white person to pose in any mantle of power or authority; for this death gave the lie to both of them.

And this death would go on too, for nothing less than the reform of a society would bring it to an end. It was the menace of the socially frustrated, strangers to mercy, striking like adders for the dark reasons of ancient minds, at any who crossed their paths.

About the Author

Alan Paton, a citizen of South Africa, achieved international fame in 1948 with the publication of *Cry, the Beloved Country*, a novel dealing with racial problems in his own country, where the government pursues an official policy of segregation and repression of black people.

Although he is himself a white man, Alan Paton chose, on graduation from college, to devote himself to the cause of black people. "I was no longer a white person," he said, "but a member of the human race." In 1935 he became the principal of a reformatory for black juvenile delinquents where he earned a considerable reputation for the changes he introduced, allowing the boys more freedom and encouraging them to live a better life when they left. "Death of a Tsotsi" is based on his experiences at the reformatory.

Alan Paton became president of the Liberal party in South Africa in 1953. Because this party advocated equal rights for black people, it was recently abolished by the government. Today Mr. Paton is forbidden to leave his country.

FOR DISCUSSION

"Death of a Tsotsi" is another story of theme. To understand this theme, we must take into account not only the plot and the characters, but also the setting—the environment in which Spike grew up and lived.

Understanding the Setting

1. What hints are offered in the story regarding the life Spike must have led before he got to the reformatory?

2. Does the reformatory strike you as a good place for juvenile criminals, or as a bad place? Support your answer by references to the content of the story.

3. What hints does the story give about the living conditions of black people in the city that Spike went back to after his dismissal from the reformatory?

126 Understanding the Characters

1. Does Spike at the beginning of the story seem to be a likable boy, or do you tend to dislike him? Explain why you feel as you do.

 2. Reread that part of the story which deals with the fight Spike had with Walter (pages 117 to 118).

a. Why was Walter's remark about Spike's being "reformed" viewed as an insult? What did Walter evidently mean?

b. What did the principal (the narrator) mean when he said that Spike, in being reformed, was "going forward to being a man"?

c. Who do *you* think was right about Spike's reform, the principal or Walter?

3. What opinion do you have of the principal's way of running a reformatory?

4. How was the Spike who left the reformatory different from the old Spike who had entered the reformatory? In this connection, explain whether you think Spike decided to carry a knife or not.

5. What are your impressions of the boy Walter? Why does he say so little when the principal tells him of Spike's death? In this connection, explain this sentence:
"Between him and me there was an unbridgeable chasm; so far as I know there was nothing in the world, not one hurt or grievance or jest or sorrow, that could have stirred us both together."

Understanding the Theme

The theme of this story is the product of the combination of story, setting, and characters. It is summed up in the last two paragraphs, particularly in the last sentence.

Before you answer the questions, reread these two paragraphs and study the last sentence carefully. (People who are "socially frustrated" are those who cannot get anywhere in life because their society and living conditions hold them back.)

1. Was the killing of Spike the result of a private gang **127** quarrel or of something more important? Support your answer by references to the content of the story.

2. If you think the killing was the result of something bigger, explain what you think the cause really was.

3. The story doesn't definitely tell us how such crimes can be prevented, but it does offer a hint. What hint is offered at the end of the story as to how such crimes may be eliminated in the future?

4. This story takes place in South Africa. Do the events in the story and the theme have any connection with events and problems in our country? Explain your answer.

VOCABULARY GROWTH

Some unfamiliar words in this story are important in understanding the characters and the theme. Most often, the context is helpful in getting the meaning.

Each of these words is first offered below in the original context in which it appeared in the story. Then it is offered in another sentence to help you further in understanding the meaning. Read both sentences. Then select the best meaning from the four choices offered, making sure the meaning you select fits the context.

1. *drab*
   A. "The khaki shirts and shorts of the reformatory were too *drab* for him, and he had a red scarf and yellow handkerchief which he arranged to peep out of his shirt pocket."
   B. Her clothes never attracted attention because they were so colorless and *drab*.

   a. dull **b.** wet **c.** poorly made **d.** poorly fitted

2. *enigmatic*
   A. "He wore the red scarf on all occasions, saying with an earnest expression that turned into an *enigmatic* smile . . . that his throat was sore."

B. His expression was so *enigmatic* that you couldn't tell whether he was angry or sad or happy.

   a. joyful   **b.** stupid   **c.** puzzling   **d.** obvious

3. *morose*

   A. "He (George) is *morose* and sullen."

   B. Because of his anger at his misfortunes, he has a *morose* feeling about the world.

   a. optimistic   **b.** easy-going   **c.** lacking in interest
   d. sour in mood

4. *sullen*

   A. "He is morose and *sullen*."

   B. After the severe scolding by his mother, he walked about in a *sullen* mood.

   a. sulky   **b.** playful   **c.** sincere   **d.** impetuous

5. *elated*

   A. "When a boy leaves the reformatory, he is usually *elated*, and does not hide his high spirits. But Spike was subdued."

   B. I was *elated* to hear I had got a grade of 100 in my final test.

   a. emphatic   **b.** serious   **c.** free from fear
   d. very joyful

FOR COMPOSITION

1. Do you know of anyone who early in his life did bad or wrong things but somehow turned out well? Tell about that person and explain why he or she changed.

2. Crime seems to be increasing among young people. Write a composition in which you explain why you think this is so.

3. Do you think young criminals should be given severe punishment, or do you favor other treatment? Explain your ideas in a composition.

4. Do you think that prejudice and discrimination cause some people to turn to crime? Explain your ideas.

TWO STORIES
OF
THE WEST

TWO STORIES
OF
THE WEST

Midnight

WILL JAMES

The cowpuncher in this story loved wild horses,
especially the wildest and proudest of them all, the
horse called Midnight. He showed his love in a
way that may seem unusual indeed.

RUNNING MUSTANGS had got to be an old game
for me; it'd got so that instead of getting some pleasure and
excitement out of seeing a wild bunch running smooth into
our trap corrals I was finding myself wishing they'd break
through the wings and get away.

Now that was no way for a mustang runner to feel but
I figgered I just loved horses too well, and thinking it over
I was kind of glad I felt that way. I seen that the money I'd
get out of the sales of 'em didn't matter so much to me as
the liberty I was helping take away from the slick wild studs,
mares, and specially the little colts. Yes, sir, it was like
getting blood money only worse.

I may be called chicken-hearted and all that but it's
my feelings, and them same feelings come from *knowing*
horses, and being with 'em steady enough so I near savvy
horse language. My first light of day was split by the shape

of a horse tied back of the wagon I was born in, and from then on horses was my main interest.

I'd got to be a good rider, and as I roamed the countries of the United States, Mexico and Canada, riding for the big cow and horse outfits of them countries I rode many a different horse in as many a different place and fix. There was times when the horse under me meant my life, specially once in Old Mexico, that once I sure can't forget, and then again, crossing the deserts I did cross, most always in strange territory and no arrows pointing as to the whereabouts of moisture, I had to depend altogether on the good horse under me wether the next water was twelve or sometimes forty-eight hours away.

With all the rambling I done which was for no reason at all only to fill the craving of a cowpuncher what always wanted to drift over that blue ridge ahead, my life was pretty well with my horse and I found as I covered the country, met different folks, and seen many towns, that the pin-eared pony under me (whichever one it was) was a powerful friend, powerful in confidence and strength. There was no suspicious question asked by him, nor "when do we eat." His rambling qualities was all mine to use as I seen fit, and I never abused it which is why I can say that I never was set afoot. Sometimes I had horses that was sort of fidgety and was told they'd leave me first chance they got wether they was hobbled or not but somehow I never was left, not even when the feed was scattered and no water for 'em to drink, and I've had a few ponies on such long cross-country trails that stayed close to camp with nothing on 'em that'd hinder 'em from hitting out if they wanted to.

A horse got to mean a heap more to me than just an animal to carry me around, he got to be my friend, I went

131

fifty-fifty with him, and even though some showed me fight and I treated 'em a little rough there'd come a time when we'd have an understanding and we'd agree that we was both pretty good fellers after all.

And now that things are explained some, it all may be understood why running mustangs, catching 'em, and selling 'em to any hombre that wanted 'em kind of got under my skin and where I live. I didn't see why I should help catch and make slaves out of them wild ones that was so free. Any and all of 'em was my friends—they was horseflesh.

The boys wasn't at all pleased when I told 'em I'd decided to leave and wanted to know why, but I kept my sentiments to myself and remarked that I'd like to go riding for a cow outfit for a change. That seemed to satisfy 'em some and when they see I was bound to go they didn't argue. We started to divvy up the amount of ponies caught so as I'd get my share, and figgered fourteen head was coming to me. There was two days' catch already in the round corral of the trap and from that little bunch we picked out them I was to get.

There was a black stud in that bunch that I couldn't help but notice—I'd kept track of him ever since he was spotted the day before. He was young and all horse, and acted like he had his full share of brains. I wondered some how he come to get caught, and then again I had to size up the trap noticing how easy a horse, even a human, could be fooled, so well we'd built it.

The big main corral took in over an acre of ground; the fine, strong woven wire fastened on the junipers and piñons wasn't at all to be seen, specially by horses going at full speed, and the strength and height of that fence would of held a herd of stampeding buffalo.

Knowing that trap as I did, it was no wonder after all
that black horse *was* caught. Nothing against his thinking
ability, I thought, and as I watches him moving around
wild-eyed seeming like to take a last long look at the steep
hills he knowed so well I finds myself saying, "Little horse,
I'm daggone sorry I helped catch you."

Right then I wanted that black horse, and I was sure
going to get him if I could. I maneuvers around a lot and
finally decides to offer the boys any three of the wild ones
that'd been turned over to me as my share in trade for the
black. It took a lot of persuading, 'cause that black stud
ranked way above the average, but the boys seeing that I
wanted him so bad and me offering one more horse for him
which made four, thought best to let me have. him.

It was early the next morning when the black and the
other ten horses I still had left was started away from the
trap. Three of the boys was helping me keep 'em together,
and as the wild ones all had to have one front foot tied up,
it hindered 'em considerable to go faster than a walk, but
that's what we wanted. We traveled slow and steady. The
ponies tried to get away often, but always there was a rider
keeping up with 'em on easy lope, and they finally seen where
they had to give in and travel along the way *we* wanted 'em.

Fifteen miles or so away from the trap and going over
a low summit, we get sight of a small high-fenced pasture,
and to one side was the corrals. There was a cabin against
the aspens and as I takes in the layout I recognizes it to be
one of the Three T's Cattle Company's cow camps.

I decided we'd gone far enough with them horses for
one day, so we corralled 'em there, and the boys went back
after me telling 'em the ponies was herd-broke enough
so I could handle 'em the next day by my lonesome, but

134 they was some dubious about one man being able to do all that, even *if* the wild ones was tired, one foot tied up, and not aching to run.

The cabin was deserted, and I was glad of it, for I wasn't wanting company right then, I wanted to think. I went to sleep thinking and dreamt I was catching wild horses by the hundreds, and selling 'em to big slough-footed "hawn-yawks" what started beating 'em over the heads with clubs. I caught one big white stud and he just followed me in the trap. It all struck me as too easy to catch 'em, and the little money I was getting for 'em turned out to be a scab on my feelings compared to the price freedom was worth to them ponies.

I woke up early next morning and the memory of that dream was still with me, and when I pulled on my boots, built a fire and put on the coffee, I had visions of that black horse in the corral looking through a collar and pulling a plow in Alabama or some other such country.

I went outside, and while waiting for the coffee to come to a boil I struts out to the corral to take a look at the ponies. They're all bunched up, heads down, and ganted up, but soon as they see me they start milling, all heads up and a-snorting. I looks through the corral bars at 'em and watches 'em.

The black stud is closest to me and kinda protecting the mares and younger stock, there's a look in his eye that kinda reminds me of a man waiting for a sentence from the judge, only the spirit is still there and mighty challenging the same as to say, "What did I do?"

A little two-year-old filly slides up alongside of him and stares at me. I can see fear in her eyes and a kinda innocent wondering as to what this was all about, this being run into a trap, roped, a foot tied up, and then drove into another place with *bars* around.

All is quiet for a spell in the corral, a meadow lark is tuning up on a fence post close by, and with the light morning breeze coming through the junipers and piñons there's a feeling for everything that lives to just sun itself, listen, and breathe in.

Then it came to me how one time I'd got so homesick for just what I was experiencing right then, the country, and everything that was in it—I'd been East to a big town and got stranded there—that I'd given my right arm just so I got back.

When I come to and looked back in the corral, the black horse was looking way over the bars to the top of a big ridge. Out there was a small bunch of mustangs enjoying their freedom for all they was worth. So far there was no chance of a collar for them, and wether it was imagination or plain facts that I could see in that black stud's face, I sure made it out that he understood all that he was seeing was *past*, the shady junipers, the mountain streams, green grass and white sage was all to be left behind, even his little bunch of mares was going to be separated from him and took to goodness knows where.

Yes, sir! Thinking it all over that way sure made it hard to take. I didn't want to get sentimental, but daggone it I couldn't help but realize that I was the judge sentencing 'em to confinement and hard labor just for the few lousy dollars they'd bring.

Sure enough, *I* was the judge and could do as I blamed please. It struck me queer that it didn't come to me sooner.

I wasn't hesitating none as I picked up my rope and opened the gate into the corral, I worked fast as I caught

136   each wild one, throwed him and took off the rope that was fastened from the tail to the front foot.

They was all foot-loose excepting the black. I hadn't passed judgment on him as yet, but I knowed he wasn't going to be shipped to no cotton field, and the worst that could come his way would be to break him for my own saddle horse.

I opened the corral gate and lets the others out, watches 'em a spell, then turns to watch the black. "Little horse," I says to him, "your good looks and build are against you—"

But it was sure hard to let the others go and keep him in that way, it didn't seem square and the little horse was sure worrying about his bunch leaving him all by his lonesome, in a big corral with a human, and then I thinks of all the saddle horses I already had, of all the others I could get that's been raised under fence and never knowed wild freedom.

Then my rope sings out once more, in no time his front foot is loose, the gate is open, and nothing in front of him but the high ridges of the country he knowed so well.

For a second I feel like kicking myself for letting such a horse go. He left me and the corral seemed like without touching the earth, floating out a ways, then turned and stood on his tiptoes, shook his head at me, let out a long whistle the same as to say "this is sure a surprise" and away he went, right on the trail his mares had took.

My heart went up my throat for a minute, I'd never seen a prettier picture to look at than that horse when he ambled away. The sight of him didn't seem to fit in with a saddle on his back, and a heap less with a collar around his neck and following furrows instead of the mountain trails he was to run on once more.

I felt some relieved and thankful as I started back for 137
the cabin. The coffee had boiled over while I was at the
corral, and put the fire out, but I finds myself whistling
and plumb contented with everything in general as I gathers
kindling and starts the fire once again.

It was a few days later when I rides in on one of the
Three T's round-up wagons, gets a job, a good string of company ponies, and goes to work. The wagon was on a big
circle and making a new camp every day towards the mustang territory.

I was trying to get used to riding for a cow outfit once
more, and it was hard. I'd find myself hankering to run
mustangs but then I'd see them wild ponies crowded into
stock cars and my hankering would die down sudden.

One day a couple of the boys rode up to the parada (main
herd) from circle with a very few head of stock and it set
me to wondering how come their horses could be so tired
in that half-a-day's ride, but I didn't have to wonder long,
for soon as they got near me one of 'em says, "We seen him!"

"Seen who?" I asks.

"Why, that black stud Midnight. Ain't you ever heard
of him?"

"I don't know," I says, but it wasn't just a few minutes
till I did know.

From all I was told right then it seemed like that Midnight horse was sure a wonder. It was rumored he was at
least a half standard, but nobody was worried about that,
the main thing was that he could sure run and what's
more, keep it up.

"We spotted him early this morning," says one of the
boys, "and soon as we did we naturally forgot all about
cows. We took turns relaying on him. We had fast horses

too, but we'd just as well tried to relay after a runaway locomotive."

I learned he had been caught once and broke to ride, but his mammy was a mustang, he'd been born and raised on the high pinnacles of the wild horse country, and one day when his owner thought it was safe to turn him out in a small pasture for a chance at green grass the horse just up and disappeared. The fences he had to cross to the open country never seemed to hinder him, and even though he was some three hundred miles from his home range, it was but a week or so later when some rider spotted him there again.

A two hundred dollar reward was offered for anyone that caught him. Many a good horse was tired out by different riders trying to get near him, traps was built, but Midnight had been caught once, and the supposed-to-be-wise fox was dumb compared to that horse.

I was getting right curious about then, and finally I asks for a full description of that flying hunk of horseflesh.

I'm holding my breath some as I'm told that his weight is around eleven hundred, pure black, and perfect built, and a small brand on his neck right under his mane, a "C."

Yep! that was him, none other than that black horse I turned loose.

I started wondering how *we* caught him so easy, but a vision of that trap came to me again. It wasn't at all like the traps other mustangers of that country ever built, and that's what got Midnight. We had him thinking he was getting away from us easy, when at the same time he was running right inside the strong, invisible net fence.

A picture of him came to my mind as he looked when I turned him loose that day now a couple of weeks past, and then I thought of the two hundred that was offered to any-body who'd run him in. That was a lot of money for a mustang, but somehow it didn't seem to be much after all, not comparing with Midnight.

It was late in the fall when I seen the black stud again. Him and his little bunch was sunning themselves on the side of a high ridge. A sarvisberry bush was between me and them, and tying my horse to a juniper, I sneaks up towards 'em, making sure to keep out of sight. I figgered I'd be about two hundred yards from the bunch once I got near the berry bush, but when I got there and straightened up to take a peek through the branches, the wild bunch had plumb evaporated off the earth. I could see for a mile around me but all I could tell of the whereabouts of Midnight and his mares was a light dust away around the point of the ridge.

"Pretty wise horse," I thinks, but somehow I felt relieved a lot to know he was going to make himself mighty hard to catch.

The winter that came was a tough one, the snow was deep and grass was hard to get. I was still riding for the Three T's outfit and was kept mighty busy bringing whatever stock I'd find what needed feed, and as I was riding the country for such and making trails out for snowbound cattle I had a good chance to watch how the wild horses was making it.

They wasn't making it very good, and as the already long winter seemed to never want to break I noticed that the bunches was getting smaller, many of the old mares layed down never to get up, and the cayotes was getting fat.

Midnight and his bunch was nowheres to be seen, and I got kind of worried that some hombre wanting that two hundred dollars right bad had started out after him with

140 grain-fed horses, and the black horse being kinda weaker on account of the grass being hard to get at might've let a rope sneak up on him and draw up around his neck.

I knowed of quite a few riders that calculated to get him that winter, and I knowed that if he wasn't already caught, he'd sure been fogged a good many times.

I often wished that I'd hung on to him while I had him, and give him as much freedom as I could, just so nobody pestered him. I'd forgot that the horse already belonged to somebody else and I'd have to give him up anyway, but that pony had got under my skin pretty deep. I just wanted to do a good turn to horseflesh in general by leaving him and all the other wild ones as they was.

Winter finally broke up and spring with warm weather had come, when as I'm riding along one day tailing up weak stock, I finds that all my worries about the black stud getting caught was for nothing.

I was in the bottom of a boggy wash helping a bellering critter up on her feet. As luck would have it my horse was hid, and as for me, only my head was sticking up above the bank, when I happened to notice the little wild bunch filing in towards me from over a low ridge. I recognized Midnight's mares by their color and markings, but I couldn't make out that shaggy, faded, long-haired horse trailing in along behind quite a ways. He was kind of a dirty brown.

I stood there in the mud up above my ankles and plumb forgot the wild-eyed cow that was so much in need of a boost to dry ground, all my interest was for spotting Midnight, and my heart went up my throat as I noticed the faded brown horse. That couldn't be Midnight, I thought, Midnight must of got caught some way and this shadow of a horse just naturally appropriated the bunch.

But as I keeps on watching 'em train in and getting closer there's points about that shaggy pony in the rear that strikes me familiar. He looks barely able to pack his own weight, and his weight wasn't much right then for I could see his ribs mighty plain even through the long winter hair. All the other ponies had started to shed off some and was halfways slick, but not him.

The bunch was only a couple of ropes' length away from me as they trailed in the boggy wash to get a drink of the snow water, and I had to hug the bank to keep out of sight and stick my head in a sagebrush so as I could see without them seeing me.

Then I recognized Midnight. That poor son of a gun was sure well disguised with whatever ailed him, and when I got a good look at that head of his I thought sure a rattler had bit him. His jaws and throat was all swelled up plumb to his ears, but as I studies him I seen it wasn't a snake's doings. It was distemper at its worst, and the end was as sure as if he'd been dead unless I could catch him and take care of him.

I'm out on my best horse the next morning, and making sure the corral gate was wide open and the wings to it in good shape I headed for the quickest way of locating Midnight. I had no trouble there, and run onto him and his bunch when only a couple of hours away from camp.

I thought he was weak enough so I could ride right in on him and rope him on the spot, but I was fooled mighty bad. He left me like I was standing still, and tail up he headed for the roughest country he could find, me right after him.

My horse was grain-fed, steady, strong, and in fine shape to run, but as the running kept up over washouts,

142 mountains, and steep ridges for the big part of that day, I
seen where there was less hope of ever getting within roping
distance of the black.

Daggone that horse anyway. I was finding myself cussing
and admiring him at the same time. I was afraid he'd run
himself to death rather than let any rider get near him, and
I thought some of letting him go, only I knowed the distemper would kill him sure, and I wanted to save him.

I made a big circle and covered a lot of territory, my horse
was getting mighty tired, and as I pushed on the trail of
Midnight and got to within a few miles of my camp, I
branched off and let him go. I was going to get me a fresh
horse.

I was on his trail again by sundown, and an hour or so
later a big moon came up to help me keep track of the dust
Midnight was making. That big moon was near halfways up
the sky when I begins to see signs of the black horse weaken-
ing. I feels mighty sorry for the poor devil right then, and as
I uncoils my rope and gets ready to dab it on him I says to
him, "Midnight, old horse, I'm only trying to help you."

Then my rope sails out and snares him. He didn't fight
as I drawed up my slack and stopped him, instead his head
hung down near the ground and if I ever seen a picture
marking the end of the trail, there was one.

It was daybreak as we finally reached the corral and
sheds of my camp. In a short while I'd lanced and doctored
up his throat, good as any vet could of done, made him
swallow a good stiff dose of medicine I had on hand for that
purpose in case any of my ponies ever got layed up that
way, and seeing he had plenty to eat and drink in case he'd
want it I started towards the cabin to cook me a bait. That
done and consumed I caught me another fresh horse and
rode out for that day's work.

I'd been doctoring up on Midnight for a week without 143
sign he ever would recuperate. He was the same as the day
I brought him in and I was getting scared that he never
would come out of it. Every night and morning as I'd go
to give him his medicine I'd stand there and watch him for
a spell. He'd got used to that and being that my visits that
way meant some relief to his suffering he got to looking for
me, and would nicker kinda soft as he'd get sight of me.

If I could only get him to eat the grain I'd bring there'd
be a chance but he didn't seem to know what grain was,
and from that I got the idea he hadn't been treated any too
well that first time he was caught. I'd kept sprinkling some
of that grain in the hay so as he'd get used to the taste and
begin looking for it, but he wasn't eating much hay and it
took quite a long time before I begin noticing that the grain
I'd put in the box had been touched. From then on, he
started eating it and gradually got so he'd clean up all I'd
give him.

There was the beginning of a big change in the little
horse after that. The powders I'd mix in the grain started
to working on him, the swelling on his neck went down, his
eyes showed brighter, and he begin to shed the long faded
winter hair. After that it was easy, a couple of weeks more
care and he was strong as ever again, all he needed was the
green grass that was all over hills by now. It was time for
me to turn him loose—and that's what I did.

It was near sundown when I let him out from under the shed, through the corral where I'd let him out
of once before near a year past, and on out to where
he'd be free to go. I took the hackamore off his head—
nothing was holding him—but this time he just stood there,
his head was high and his eyes was taking in the big
country around him.

He spoke plainer than a human when, after taking long appreciating breaths of the cool spring air, he sniffed at my shoulder and looked up the hills again. He wasn't wondering or caring if I understood him so long as he understood me, and that he did—he knowed I was with him for all the freedom these valleys and mountains could give him.

It was a couple of months later when one of the cowboys rode up to my camp on his way to the home ranch, stopped with me a night, and before he left the next morning dropped me some information that caused me to do a heap of thinking.

It appeared like some outfit had moved in on this range and was going to clean it out of all the wild horses that was on it. They had permits and contracts to do that and seemed like the capital to go through with it. Most of 'em were foreign hombres that craved for other excitements than just jazz, and getting tired of spending their old man's money all in one place had framed it up to come West and do all that *for a change*.

They was bringing along some fast thoroughbreds, and I couldn't help but wonder how long them poor spindle-legged ponies would last in these rocks and shale. They'd be as helpless as the hombres riding 'em. If it'd been only them highbloods I'd just laughed and felt mighty safe for the wild ones, but no such luck, they was paying top wages and hiring the best mustang runners in the country.

As I heard it from that cowboy it was sure some expensive layout, there was big wagonloads of fancy grub and fancier drinks, air mattresses and pillows, tents and folding bathtubs and tables, perfume and chewing gum, etc., etc.— Yep! they was going to *rough it*.

"But I'm thinking," says the cowboy as he left, "that with the wild horse hunters they hired, that black stud

Midnight is going to find hisself in a trap once more, and somehow I'd kinda hate to see them catch that horse."

For a few weeks that outfit was busy building traps. I seen they was going at it big as I rode through one of 'em one day, and as I talked to one of the pilgrims who I'd found busy picking woodticks out of his brand-new Angora chaps, I also seen they had big visions of cleaning this country of the mustangs along with making a potful of money.

"And it's the greatest sport I know of," says that hombre as he reaches for another woodtick next to his ear.

"Yeh," I says to myself as I rides away, "I'm not wishing him harm, but I hope he breaks his neck at it."

There was in the neighborhood of a thousand head of mustangs in that country, and it wasn't long when the hills and white sage flats was being tore by running hoofs, a steady haze of fine dust was floating in the air and could be seen for miles around, and at night I could see signal fires. Some greenhorn had got lost or set afoot.

The hired mustang runners was having a hard time of it; one told me one day they'd of caught twice as many if them pilgrims wasn't around. "Two of the boys was bringing in a nice bunch yesterday," he was saying. "They had 'em to within a few yards of the gate and as good as caught, when up from behind a rock jumps a pilgrim and hollers, 'That's the good boys, step on 'em!' Well, the ponies turned quicker than a flash and *they* done all the stepping, a good thirty head got away."

I was glad to hear that in a way, but I was careful not to show it. I was thinking that after all Midnight and his little bunch had a chance at their freedom, and I finds myself whistling a pretty lively tune as I rode on.

I hadn't seen Midnight only once since I turned him loose that last time, and I had a hunch that he'd changed his range on account of these mustangers keeping him on the dodge, but then again this wasn't the only outfit that was out for the wild ones. The whole country for a hundred miles around was full of riders out for the fuzztails (mustangs), and I couldn't figger out where that horse and his little bunch could go where they'd be safe.

But nobody had seen the black stud, and everybody was wanting him. I was asked often if I'd seen any sign of him, and as I'd go on a-riding the country keeping tab on the company's cattle that was on the same range as the wild ones, I was watching steady for him, but he couldn't be seen anywheres.

Come a time when it was easy to notice that the mustangs was fast disappearing. I could ride for a week at a stretch without seeing more than a few head where some months before I could of counted hundreds. I'd run acrost little colts, too young to keep up and left behind. Their mammies had stayed with 'em long as they could but as the riders would gain on 'em fast, fear would get the best of 'em, and the poor little devils would be left behind to shift for themselves before they was able to, and keep a-nickering and a-circling for the mammy that never came back. She'd be in the trap.

Carloads of wild ones was being shipped every month to all points of the U. S. wherever there was a market for 'em. They was sold to farmers and drug to the farm back of a wagon, the trip in the stock cars, not mentioning their experiences in the trap, took most of the heart out of 'em, and there was no fight much as the collar was slipped around their necks and hooked up alongside the gentle farm horse— a big change from the tall peaks, mountain streams near hid with quaking asp, bunch grass, and white sage.

It was late fall and the air was getting mighty crimpy when the mustang-running outfits started pulling up their tent pins and moving out, the country looked mighty silent and deserted and all the black dots that could be seen at a distance wasn't mustangs no more, it was mighty safe to say that them black dots was cattle. . . .

I rides up to the pilgrim camp one day just as one of 'em is putting away his cold-cream and snake-bite outfit, and inquires how they all enjoyed the country and mustang trapping.

"Oh, the country is great, and mustang trapping is a ripping sport," I'm told, "but we lost a few thousand dollars on the deal which don't make it so good. Besides our blooded horses are ruined.

"And by the way," goes on that same hombre, "have you seen that black stallion they call Midnight anywheres? I see by the San Jacinto *News* that the reward on the horse is withdrawn, also the ownership, so he is free to anyone who catches him, I understand."

"Yes," I says, tickled to death at the news, "but there's a catch to it and that's *catching him.*"

"Free to anyone who catches him," stayed in my mind for a good many days, but where could that son of a gun be? I tried to think of all the hiding spots there was, I knowed 'em all well, I thought, but I also knowed that all them hiding spots had been rode into and the mustangs there had been caught. I was getting mighty worried that Midnight and his little bunch might by now be somewheres where the fences are thick and the fields are small, a couple of thousand miles away.

It's early one morning when I notices one of my saddle horses had got through the pasture fence and left. Soon I

148 was on his trail to bring him back, and that trail led through the aspens back of my cabin and on up to a big granite ledge where it was lost on the rocky ground. Figgering on making a short cut to where I can spot that pony, I leaves my horse tied to a buckbrush and climbs over the granite ledge. When I gets up there, there's another ledge, and then another one, and by the time I gets to the top of all of 'em I'm pretty high.

I was some surprised to find a spring up there, fine clear water that run only a short ways and sunk in the ground again, but what surprised me most was the horse tracks around it. How could a horse ever get up here, I thought, but they were here sure enough. I noticed the feed was awful short and scarce and I wondered if it was because them horses couldn't get down as easy as they got up.

Investigating around and looking over big granite boulders I can make out horses' backs a-shining in the sun. They're feeding in their small territory, and I can tell they're feeling pretty safe, but as I moves around, a head comes up, ears pointed my way, and wild eyes a staring at me.

In that second I recognized the black stud Midnight.

There's a loud snort and whistle, and like a bunch of quail Midnight and his bunch left that spot for higher ground and where they could see all around 'em, but a man afoot was something new and not so much to run away from, and finally they stood off at a good distance and watched me.

The surprise of finding Midnight, and so close to my camp, left me able to do nothing but set where I was and do my share of watching. In a little while I started talking to him and I could see he sure remembered and recognized me. His wild look disappeared and he made a half circle as if to come my way. I wished he'd come closer, but I hadn't broke him to that. I hadn't broke him to anything, I'd only

tried to give him to understand that he was safe of that freedom as long as he lived.

I knowed he understood ever since that second time I turned him loose. The proof of that was him picking his hiding place as close to my camp as he could get while the mustang runners was in the country. I know he'd been there all the last few months, and I know there was many a time when he looked down on my cabin, which was only half a mile or so away, while I was wondering where he could be.

I seen him looking down at me that way the next morning. He was hard to see amongst the scrub mahogany, but it's a wonder, I thought, why it never come to me to look up there.

Somehow or other, Midnight and his bunch got down off their hiding place. The mustang runners had all left the country, and as I rode up on the small bunch of remaining wild ones one day and watched 'em lope away toward the flat, I knowed they was safe.

I knowed they'd come back if they ever got crowded, and to that hiding place which nobody else knowed of but us 'uns.

About the Author

Will James was born in Montana in 1892, and died in 1942. All his life he loved the West—its cowboys and horses. He was adopted by a French-Canadian prospector when his parents died, and he learned from his guardian to love nature and the outdoors. He never went to school.

His guardian died when Will was fourteen years old. At that point, he made his own living at cowpunching and breaking in horses, like the narrator of "Midnight." He discovered a talent for art and wrote several illustrated articles about horses, which were published in national magazines. He followed this activity with the writing of short stories which proved very successful.

150 Two of his stories were filmed in Hollywood. In appearance Will James was always the typical cowboy—tall, rangy, deeply tanned.

FOR DISCUSSION

Understanding the Story

"Midnight" is about cowboys and horses; it is a "western" story, but not like the typical "westerns" you get in the movies or on the TV screen. With some changes, it might have been a typical western. What we want to consider is how this story differs, specifically, from westerns you are more familiar with, and why the author chose to write it as he did.

1. The chief difference between mature fiction in general and most juvenile and popular fiction is that in the former, the characters will act in all circumstances as such people *would* really act; in most TV and moving picture westerns, the characters act as the viewers *like* them to act in order to get thrills and happy endings.

   a. In real life, what would a sheriff probably do if he found that he had met with a band of fifteen outlaws?

   b. In the typical TV show or moving picture, what does this sheriff do?

2. At what points in the story "Midnight" would a typical TV writer make changes in order to please his audience? What changes would he make?

3. Now let us consider why Will James, the author, wrote his story as he did.

a. The cowpuncher who tells the story (the narrator) and the horse Midnight have characters that are in many respects alike. How are they alike?

b. This likeness in character serves in the story both to draw them together and at the same time to keep them apart. Can you explain this statement and illustrate it by referring to the events in the story?

4. The Easterners are interestingly described on pages 144 and 145. Note particularly their reasons for coming and their equipment for "roughing it." What comparisons would you make between them and the narrator of the story?

A pilgrim is one who travels great distances to visit a holy place. Why do you suppose the cowboys called these Easterners "pilgrims"?

5. Two changes in a TV version of this story—changes you probably thought of in answering question 2—would probably occur when the cowboy cures Midnight of his illness, and at the close when he lets Midnight go for the last time.

Taking into consideration the characters of the cowboy, Midnight, and the Easterners, explain why you think the author, Will James, was *right* or *wrong* in writing the story as he did at each of these two points.

6. Do you think the story has a happy or an unhappy ending? Keep in mind the probable future of the two main characters. In this connection, what significance may there be in the fact that Midnight's final hiding place is so high and difficult to get to, and yet so close to his cowboy friend?

Understanding the Author's Art

The language in which this story is written is full of misspellings and mistakes in grammar. Did you notice them?

The story might have been told in different language. The second paragraph might have been written as follows:

Simpson (a name for the mustang runner) knew that no mustang runner ought to feel as he did, but he was helpless; he loved horses too much, and, on deliberation, he was happy that he felt as he did. He was aware that the profits secured from transactions in horseflesh mattered less to him than the liberty which the wild studs, the mares, especially the little colts would be deprived of. Indeed, he was inclined to look upon his profits as blood money.

1. Compare this version with the original second paragraph. Is the story better as Will James wrote it, or would it be better written in more elegant and correct language? Think of several reasons to support your opinion.

2. Aside from the question of the language used, how was your interest in the story influenced by the fact that it was told in the first person?

VOCABULARY GROWTH

Appreciating the Author's Use of Words

As rough as this westerner's language may have sounded, he was very good in using words that gave clear and interesting pictures of some of the characters, places, and events of the story. The ability to use words that give clear and exact rather than vague impressions is one that all of us should try to develop. Look up (in your dictionary) each of the italicized words or expressions in these sentences from the story, and be ready to explain the exact picture the writer was conveying.

1. "...and dreamt I was catching wild horses by the hundreds, and selling 'em to big *slough-footed* 'hawn-yawks' what started beating 'em over the heads with clubs."

2. "...I'd never seen a prettier picture to look at than that horse [Midnight] when he *ambled* away."

3. "The sight of him didn't seem to fit in with...a collar around his neck and following *furrows* instead of mountain trails...." (What kind of *furrows* would these be?)

4. "... he'd been born and raised on the high *pinnacles* 153 of the wild horse country...." (What picture of Midnight do you get?)

5. "... but when I got there and straightened up to take a peek through the branches, the wild bunch [the horses] had plumb *evaporated* off the earth." (Think of what happens when water *evaporates*. What picture do you get?)

6. "I was in the bottom of a *boggy wash* helping a bellering critter [a cow] up on her feet." (Which of the dictionary meanings of *wash* makes sense here? How does *boggy* add to the picture?)

FOR COMPOSITION

1. Did Midnight remind you of any animal you know in real life? Describe that animal and some of his behavior that makes him resemble Midnight.

2. Some people have the same need for freedom and independence that the narrator had; they cannot stand confinement and rules. If you know such a person, tell about him, and illustrate your point with examples of his behavior.

3. Have you seen a TV or moving picture "western" in which the characters seemed more realistic (true-to-life) than usual? Explain why this "western" seemed more realistic, citing events in the story to prove your point.

Jacob

JACK SCHAEFER

When you think of the West a hundred
years ago, do you think of Indians and Indian
wars? What kind of people were those Indians?
This story is about a boy's brief encounter with
an Indian chief of fierce reputation.

THOSE MOCCASINS? Mine. Though I never wore
them. Had them on just once to see if they fitted. They did.
A bit tight but I could get them on.

Don't touch them. The leather's old and dry and the
stitching rotted. Ought to be. They've been hanging there
a long time. Look close and you can see the craftsmanship.
The best. They're Nez Percé moccasins. Notice the design
worked into the leather. It's faint now but you can make it
out. Don't know how they did that but the Nez Percés could
really work leather. A professor who studied such things told
me once that design means they're for a chief. For his
ceremonial appearances, sort of his dress-up footwear. Said
only a chief could use that design. But it's there. Right there
on those moccasins.

Yes. They're small. Boy size. That's because I was a boy then. But they're a chief's moccasins all the same. Kept them down the years because I'm proud of them. And because they mind me of a man. He had a red skin. Copper would be closer the color. A muddy copper. And I only saw him once. But he was a man.

That was a long way from here. A long way. In years and in miles. I was ten then, maybe eleven, maybe twelve, in that neighborhood, I disremember exactly. Best I can do is place it in the late seventies. Funny how definite things like dates and places slip away and other stray things, like the way you felt at certain times and how your first wild strawberries tasted, can remain clear and sharp in your mind. We were living, my folks and my older brother and myself, in a little town in eastern Montana. Not much of a place. Just a small settlement on the railroad that wouldn't have amounted to anything except that it had a stretch of double track where a train going one direction could pull off to let one going the other get past. My father was a switchman. Looked after track and handled the west-end switch. That was why we were there.

The Indian smell was still in the air in those days. People around here and nowadays wouldn't know what that means. It was a knowing and a remembering that not so far away were still real live free-footed fighting Indians that might take to raiding again. They were pegged on treaty lands and supposed to stay there. But they were always hot over one thing or another, settlers gnawing into their hunting grounds or agents pinching their rations or maybe the government forgetting to keep up treaty payments. You never knew when they might get to figuring they'd been

156 pushed far enough and would start council fires up in the hills and come sudden and silent out of the back trails, making trouble. It was only a year or two since the Custer affair on the Little Big Horn southwest of where we were. No one with any experience in those things expected the treaty that ended that business to hold long.

Don't take me wrong. We didn't look for Indians behind bushes and sit around shivering at night worrying about attacks. The nearest reservation was a fair jump away and if trouble started we'd know about it long before it reached us, if it ever did. Matter of fact it never did. I grew up in that territory and never once was mixed in any Indian trouble past an argument over the price of a blanket. Never even saw any fighting Indians except this once I'm telling about and then they weren't fighting any more. It was just a smell in the air, the notion there might be trouble any time. Indians were quite a topic when I was a boy and the talk of an evening chewed it plenty.

Expect I heard as much of it as any of the boys around our settlement. Maybe more. My father had been in the midst of the Sioux outbreak in Minnesota in the early sixties. He'd seen things that could harden a man. They settled his mind on the subject. "Only good Indian," he'd say, "is a dead one." Yes. That's not just a saying out of the storybooks. There were men who really said it. And believed it. My father was one. Said it and believed it and said it so often I'd not be stretching the truth past shape to figure he averaged it couple times a week and so naturally we boys believed it too, hearing it all the time. I'll not argue with anyone wants to believe it even today. I'm only telling you what happened to me.

Hearing that kind of talk we boys around the settlement had our idea what Indians were like. I can speak for myself anyway. The Indians I saw sometimes passing through on a train or loafing around a town the few times I was in one with the folks didn't count. They were tame ones. They were scrawny mostly and they hung around where white people were and traded some and begged liquor when they couldn't buy it. They weren't dangerous or even interesting. They didn't matter more'n mules or dogs or anything like that cluttering the landscape. It was the wild ones filled my mind, the fighting kind that lived the way they always had and went on the warpath, and made the government send out troops and sign treaties with them. Can't recall exactly what I thought they looked like, but they were big and fierce and dangerous and they liked to burn out homesteaders' cabins and tie people to wagon wheels and roast them alive over slow fires, and it took a brave man to go hunting them and look at them down the sights of his gun. Days I felt full of ginger I'd plan to grow up quick and be an Indian fighter. Late afternoon, before evening chores, I'd scout the country-side with the stick I used for a gun and when I'd spot a spray of red sumac poking out of a brush clump, I'd belly-it in the grass and creep to good cover and poke my gun through and draw my bead. I'd pull on the twig knob that was my trigger and watch careful, and sometimes I'd have to fire again and then I'd sit up and cut another notch on the stick. I had my private name for that. Making good Indians, I called it.

What's that got to do with those moccasins? Not much I guess. But I'm telling this my way. It's all part of what I remember when I sit back and study those moccasins a spell.

The year I'm talking about was a quiet one with the Sioux but there was some Indian trouble all right, along in the fall and a ways away, over in the Nez Percé country in Idaho. It started simple enough like those things often did.

158 There was this band lived in a valley, maybe seven hundred of them all told, counting the squaws and young ones. Biggest safe estimate I heard was three hundred braves, fighting men I mean. Can't remember the name of the valley, though I should. My brother settled there. But I can recall the name of the chief. That sticks. Always will. Not the Indian of it because that was a fancy mouthful. What it meant. Mountain Elk. Not that exactly. Big-Deer-That-Walks-the-High-Places. Mountain Elk is close enough. But people didn't call him that. Most Indians had a short name got tagged to them somehow and were called by it. His was Jacob. Sounded funny first time I heard it but not after I'd been hearing it a while.

As I say, this trouble started simple enough. We heard about it from the telegraph operator at the settlement who took his meals at our place. He picked up information relaying stuff through his key. News of all kinds and even military reports. Seems settlers began closing in around Jacob's valley and right soon began looking at the land there. Had water which was important in that country. Some of them pushed in and Jacob and his boys pushed them back out. So complaints were being made and more people wanted to move in, and talk went around that land like that was too good for Indians anyway because they didn't use it right, the way white men would, and when there was enough steam up a government man went in to see Jacob. Suggested the band would be better off living on some outside reservation. Get regular rations and have an agent to look after them. No, Jacob said, he and his were doing all right. Had been for quite a spell and expected to keep on doing the same. Sent his thanks to the Great White Chief for thinking about him but he wasn't needing any help. So after a while the pressure was stronger and another government man went in. Offered

to buy the land and move the band in style to a reservation. **159**
No, said Jacob, he and his children—he called them all his
children though he wasn't much past thirty himself—he and
his children liked their land and weren't interested in selling.
Their fathers had given up land too much in the past and
been forced to keep wandering and had found this place
when no one wanted it, and it was good and they had stayed
there. Most of them then living had been born there and
they wanted to die there too and that was that.

Well, the pressure went on building and there were
ruckuses here and yonder around the valley when some more
settlers tried moving in and a bunch of young braves got
out of hand and killed a few. So another government man
went in, this time with a soldier escort. He didn't bother
with arguing or bargaining. He told Jacob the Great White
Chief had issued a decree and this was that the whole tribe
was to be moved by such and such a date. If they went
peaceable, transportation would be provided and good rations. If they kept on being stubborn, soldiers would come
and make them move and that would be a bad business all
around. Yes, said Jacob, that would be a bad business but it
wouldn't be his doing. He and his children wouldn't have
made the storm but they would stand up to it if it came. He
had spoken and that was that.

So the days went along toward the date set which was
in the fall I'm telling about. Jacob and his band hadn't made
any preparations for leaving and the officer in charge of this
whole operation thought Jacob was bluffing and he'd just
call that bluff. He sent about four hundred soldiers under
some colonel into the valley the week before the moving
was supposed to happen, and Jacob and the others, the
whole lot of them, just faded away from their villages and off
into the mountains behind the valley. The colonel sent scout-

ing parties after them but couldn't make contact. He didn't know what to do in that situation so he set up camp there in the valley to wait and got real peeved when some of Jacob's Nez Percés slipped down out of the mountains one night and stampeded his stock. Finally he had his new orders and on the supposed moving day he carried them out. He put his men to destroying the village and they wiped it level to the ground, and the next morning early there was sharp fighting along his upper picket lines and he lost quite a few men before he could jump his troops into the field in decent force.

That was the beginning. The government wanted to open the valley for homesteading but couldn't without taking care of Jacob first. This colonel tried. He chased Jacob and his band into the mountains and thought overtaking them would be easy with the squaws and young ones slowing Jacob down, but Jacob had hidden them off somewhere and was traveling light with his braves. He led this colonel a fast run through rough country and caught him off watch a few times and whittled away at his troops every odd chance till this colonel had to turn back, not being outfitted for a real campaign. When he, that'd be this colonel, got back he found Jacob had beat him there and made things mighty unpleasant for those left holding the camp before slipping away again. About this time the government realized what it was up against and recalled the colonel and maybe whoever was his boss, and assigned a general—a brigadier—to the job and began mounting a real expedition.

We heard plenty about what happened after that, not just from the telegraph operator but from my brother who was busting the seams of his breeches those days and wanting to strike out for himself, and signed with the freighting company that got the contract carting supplies for the troops.

He didn't see any of the fighting but he was close to it several times and he wrote home what was happening. Once a week he'd promised to write and did pretty well at it. He'd send his letters along to be posted whenever any of the wagons were heading back, and my mother would read them out to my father and me when they arrived. Remember best the fat one came after he reached the first camp and saw Jacob's valley. Took him two chunks of paper both sides to tell about it. Couldn't say enough about the thick green grass and the stream tumbling into a small lake and running quiet out again, and the good trees stepping up the far slopes and the mountains climbing on to the end of time all around. Made a man want to put his feet down firm on the ground and look out steady like the standing trees and stretch tall. Expect that's why my brother quit his job soon as the trouble was over and drove his own stakes there.

Yes. I know, I'm still a long way from those moccasins. I'm over in Idaho in Jacob's valley. But I get to remembering and then I get to forgetting maybe you're not interested in all the sidelines of what I started to tell you. I'll try to move it faster.

As I was saying, the government outfitted a real expedition to go after Jacob. A brigadier general and something like a thousand men. There's no point telling all that happened except that this expedition didn't accomplish much more than the first colonel and his men did. They chased Jacob farther and almost penned him a few times and killed a lot of braves and got wind of where his women and their kids were hidden, and forced him to move them farther into the mountains with them getting out just in time, not being able to carry much with them. But that wasn't catching Jacob and stopping him and his braves from carrying on their hop-skip-and-jump war against all whites in general and these troops in

162 particular. Then a second general went in and about a thousand more soldiers with them and they had hard fighting off and on over a couple hundred miles and more, and the days drove on into deep winter and Jacob was licked. Not by the government and its soldiers and their guns. By the winter. He and his braves, what was left of them, had kept two generals and up to two thousand troops busy for four months fighting through parts of three states and then the winter licked him. He came to the second general under truce in what remained of his chief's rig and took off his headdress and laid it on the ground and spoke. His children were scattered in the mountains, he said, and the cold bit sharp and they had few blankets and no food. Several of the small ones had been found frozen to death. From the moment the sun passed overhead that day he would fight no more. If he was given time to search for his children and bring them together he would lead them wherever the Great White Chief wished.

There. I'm closer to those moccasins now even though I'm still way over in Idaho. No. Think it was in western Montana where Jacob surrendered to that second general. Well, the government decided to ship these Nez Percés to the Dump, which was what people called the Indian Territory where they chucked all the tribes whose lands weren't just cut down but were taken away altogether. That meant Jacob and his children, all that was left of them, about three hundred counting the squaws and kids, would be loaded on a special train and sent along the railroad that ran through our settlement. These Nez Percé Indians would be passing within a stone's throw of our house and we would have a chance to see them at least through the windows and maybe, if there was need for switching, the train would stop and we would have a good look.

Wonder if you can scratch up any real notion what that meant to us boys around the settlement. To me maybe most of all. These weren't tame Indians. These were wild ones. Fighting Indians. About the fightingest Indians on record. Sure, the Sioux wiped out Custer. But there were a lot more Sioux than soldiers in that scuffle. These Nez Percés had held their own mighty well against a big chunk of the whole United States Army of those days. They were so outnumbered it had got past being even a joke. Any way you figured, it had been about one brave to six or seven soldiers and those braves hadn't been well armed at the start and had to pick up guns and ammunition as they went along from soldiers they killed. Some of them were still using arrows at the finish. I'm not being funny when I tell you they kept getting bigger and fiercer in my mind all the time I was hearing about that long running fight in the mountains. It was notches for Nez Percés I was cutting on my stick now and the way I felt about them, even doing that took nerve.

The day came the train was to pass through, some time late afternoon was the first report, and all of us settlement boys stayed near the telegraph shack waiting. It was cold, though there wasn't much snow around. We'd sneaked into the shack where there was a stove, till the operator was peeved at our chattering and shooed us out, and I expect I did more than my share of the chattering because in a way these were my Indians because my brother was connected with the expedition that caught them. Don't think the other boys liked how I strutted about that. Well, anyway, the sun went down and we all had to scatter home for supper and the train hadn't come. Afterwards some of us slipped back to the shack and waited some more while the operator cussed at having to stick around waiting for word, and one by one

164 we were yanked away when our fathers came looking for us, and still the train hadn't come.

It was some time past midnight and I'd finally got to sleep when I popped up in bed at a hammering on the door. I looked into the kitchen. Father was there in his nightshirt opening the outside door and the operator was on the step cussing some more that he'd had word the train was coming, would get there in half an hour, and they'd have to switch it and hold it till the westbound night freight went past. Father added his own cussing and pulled on his pants and boots and heavy jacket and lit his lantern. By time he'd done that I had my things on too. My mother was up then and objecting, but my father thought some and shushed her. "Fool kid," he said, "excited about Indians all the time. Do him good to see what thieving smelly things they are." So I went with him. The late moon was up and we could see our way easy and I stayed in the shack with the operator and my father went off to set his signal and tend his switch. Certain enough, in about twenty minutes the train came along and swung onto the second line of track and stopped.

The telegraph operator stepped out and started talking to a brakeman. I was scared stiff. I stood in the shack doorway and looked at the train and I was shaking inside like I had some kind of fever. It wasn't much of a train. Just an engine and little fuel car and four old coaches. No caboose. Most trains had cabooses in those days because they carried a lot of brakemen. Had to have them to wrangle the hand brakes. Expect the brakeman the operator was talking to was the only one this train had. Expect that was why it was so late. I mean the railroad wasn't wasting any good equipment and any extra men on this train, and it was being shoved along slow when and as how between other trains.

I stood there shaking inside and the engine was wheezing some and the engineer and fireman were moving slow and tired around it, fussing with an oilcan and a tin of grease. That was the only sign of life I could see along the whole train. What light there was in the coaches, only one lantern lit in each, wasn't any stronger than the moonlight outside and that made the windows blank-like and I couldn't see through them. Except for the wheezing engine, that train was a tired and sleeping or dead thing on the track. Then I saw someone step down from the first coach and stretch and move into the moonlight. He was a soldier, a captain, and he looked tired and sleepy and disgusted with himself and the whole world. He pulled a cigar from a pocket and leaned against the side of the coach, lighting the cigar and blowing out smoke in a slow puff. Seeing him so lazy and casual, I stopped shaking and moved into the open and closer to the coach and shifted around trying to find an angle that would stop the light reflection on the windows and let me see in. Then I stopped still. The captain was looking at me. "Why does everybody want to gawk at them? Even kids." He took a long drag on his cigar and blew a pair of fat smoke rings. "You must want to bad," he said. "Up so late. Go on in, take a look." I stared at him, scared now two ways. I was scared to go in where those Indians were and scared not to, after he'd said I could and just about ordered I should. "Go ahead," he said. "They don't eat boys. Only girls. Only at lunchtime." And sudden I knew he was just making a tired joke, and it would be all right and I went up the steps to the front platform and peered in.

Indians. Fighting Indians. The fighting Nez Percés who had led United States soldiers a bloody chase through the mountains of three states. The big and fierce redmen who had

166 fought many times their own number of better-armed soldiers to a frequent standstill in the high passes. And they
weren't big and they weren't fierce at all. They were huddled
figures on the coach seats, two to a seat down the twin rows,
braves and squaws and young ones alike, all dusty and tired
and hunched together at the shoulders in drowsy silence or
sprawled apart over the windowsills and seat arms in sleep.
In the dim light they looked exactly like the tame Indians
I'd seen, and they seemed to shrink and shrivel even more
as I looked at them and there was no room in me for any
emotion but disappointment, and when I noticed the soldiers
sleeping in the first seats close to me I sniffed to myself at
the silly notion any guards might be needed on that train.
There wasn't the slightest hint of danger anywhere around.
Being on that train was no different from being off it except
that it was being on a stopped train and not being outside on
the ground. It didn't even take any particular nerve to do
what I did when I started walking down the aisle.

The only way I know to describe it is that I was in a sort
of trance of disappointment and I wanted to see everything
and I went straight down the aisle looking all around me.
And those Indians acted like I wasn't there at all. Those that
were awake. Each of them had his eyes fixed somewhere,
maybe out a window or at the floor or just at some point
ahead, and didn't move them. They knew I was there. I could
tell that. A feeling. A little crawling on my skin. But they
wouldn't look at me. They were somehow off away in a
place all their own and they weren't going to let me come
near getting in there with them or let me know they even
saw me outside of it. Except one. He was a young one, a boy
like me only a couple years younger, and he was scrooged
down against a sleeping brave—maybe his father—and his

small eyes, solid black in the dim light, looked at me, and **167** his head turned slow to keep them on me as I went past and I could sense them on me as I went on till the back of the seat shut them off.

Still in that funny trance I went into the next coach and through it and to the third coach and on to the last. Each was the same. Soldiers slumped in sleep, and the huddled figures of the Indians in different pairings and sprawled positions but the effect the same and then at the end of the last car I saw him. He had a seat to himself and the headdress with its red-tipped feathers hung from the rack above the seat. He was asleep with an arm along the windowsill, his head resting on it. I stopped and stared at him and the low light from the lantern near the end of the coach shone on the coppery texture of his face and the bare skin of his chest where it showed through the fallen-apart folds of the blanket wrapped around him. I stared at him and I felt cheated and empty inside. Even Jacob wasn't big or fierce. He wasn't as big as my father. He was short. Maybe broad and rather thick in the body but not much, even that way. And his face was quiet and—well, the only word I can ever think of is peaceful. I stared at him and then I started a little because he wasn't sleeping. One eyelid had twitched a bit. All at once I knew he was just pretending. He was pretending to be asleep so he wouldn't have to be so aware of the stares of anyone coming aboard to gawk at him. And sudden I felt ashamed and I hurried to the back platform to leave the train, and in the shadows there I stumbled over a sleeping soldier and heard him rousing himself as I scrambled down the steps.

That started what happened afterwards. Expect I'm really to blame for it all. Mean to say it probably wouldn't

168 have happened if I hadn't been hurrying and wakened that soldier. He didn't know I was there. He was too full of sleep at first and didn't know what had awakened him. While I stayed in the dark shadow by the coach, afraid to go out into the moonlight, he stood up and stretched and came down the steps without noticing me and went around the end of the train toward the wider shadow on the other side, and as he went I saw him pulling a bottle out of a pocket. I felt safe again and started away and turned to look back, and the light was just right for me to see some movement inside through the window by the last seat. Jacob was standing up. All kinds of wild notions poured through my mind and I couldn't move and then he was emerging through the rear door onto the platform and I wasn't exactly scared because I wasn't conscious of feeling anything at all except that I couldn't move. Time seemed to hang there motionless around me. Then I realized he wasn't doing anything and wasn't going to do anything. He wasn't even aware of me or if he was I was without meaning for him and he had seen me and dismissed me. He was standing quiet by the rear railing and his blanket was left inside and the cold night air was blowing against his bare chest above his leather breeches but he didn't appear to notice that. He was looking back along the double iron line of the track toward the tiny point of light that was my father's lantern by the west switch. He stood there, still and quiet, and I stayed where I was and watched him and he did not move and stood there looking far along the westward track and that was what we were doing, Jacob and I, when the soldier came back around the end of the train.

Thinking about it later I couldn't blame that soldier too much. Maybe had orders to keep the Indians in their seats or not let them on the rear platform or something like

that. Probably was worried about drinking on duty and not **169**
wanting to be caught letting anything slip with the tang
plain on his breath. Could be too he'd taken on more than
he could handle right. Anyway he was surprised and mad
when he saw Jacob standing there. He reached first and
pulled some object off the platform floor and when he had
it I could see it was his rifle. Then he jumped up the steps
and started prodding Jacob with the rifle barrel toward the
door. Jacob looked at him once and away and turned slow
and started to move and the soldier must have thought Jacob
moved too slow because he swung the gun around to use
the stock end like a club and smack Jacob on the back. I
couldn't see exactly what happened then because the scuffle
was too sudden and quick but there was a blur of movement
and the soldier came tumbling off the platform to the ground
near me and the gun landed beside him. He was so mad he
tripped all over himself getting to his feet and scrabbling
for the gun and he whipped it up and hip-aimed it at Jacob
and tried to fire it and the breech mechanism jammed some
way and he clawed at it to make it work.

And Jacob stood there on the platform, still and quiet
again, looking down at the soldier with bare breast broad-
side to the gun. I could see his eyes bright and black in the
moonlight and the shining on the coppery firmness of his
face and he did not move and of a sudden I realized he was
waiting. He was waiting for the bullet. He was expecting it
and waiting for it and he would not move. And I jumped
forward and grabbed the rifle barrel and pulled hard on it.
"No," I shouted. "Not like that." And the soldier stumbled
and fell against me and both of us went down and someone
was yelling at us and when I managed to get to my feet I
saw it was the captain and the soldier was up too, standing
stiff and awkward at attention. "Bloody Indian," the soldier

170 said. "Trying to get away." The captain looked up and saw Jacob standing there and jerked a bit with recognizing who it was. "He was not," I said. "He was just standing there." The captain looked at the soldier and shook his head slow. "You'd have shot that one." The captain shook his head again like he was disgusted and tired of everything and maybe even of living. "What's the use," he said. He flipped a thumb at the soldier. "Pick up your gun and get on forward." The soldier hurried off and the captain looked at Jacob and Jacob looked down at him, still and quiet and not moving a muscle. "There's fools of every color," the captain said and Jacob's eyes brightened a little as if he understood and I expect he did because I'd heard he could speak English when he wanted to. The captain wiped a hand across his face. "Stand on that damned platform as long as you want," he said. He remembered he had a cigar in his other hand and looked at it and it was out and he threw it on the ground and swung around and went toward the front of the train again, and I wanted to follow him but I couldn't because now Jacob was looking at me.

He looked down at me what seemed a long time and then he motioned at me and I could tell he wanted me to step out further into the moonlight. I did and he leaned forward to peer at me. He reached a hand out toward me, palm flat and down, and said something in his own language and for a moment I was there with him in the world that was different and beyond my own everyday world and then he swung away and stepped to stand by the rear railing again and I knew I was outside again, outside of his mind and put away and no more to him than any other object around. He was alone there looking far down the track and it sank slow and deep in me that he was looking far past the tiny light point of my father's lantern, far on where the lone track ran straight along the slow-rising reaches of distance into the horizon that led past the longest vision at last to the great climbing mountains. He was looking back along the iron trail that was taking him and his children away from a valley that would make a man want to put his feet firm on the earth and stretch tall and was taking them to an unknown place where they would not be themselves any longer but only some among many of many tribes and tongues and all dependent on the bounty of a forgetful government. It wasn't an Indian I was seeing there any more. It was a man. It wasn't Jacob, the tamed chief that even foolish kids could gawk at. It was Mountain Elk, the Big-Deer-That-Walks-the-High-Places, and he was big, really big, and he was one meant to walk the high places.

He stood there looking down the track and the west-bound night freight came rumbling out of the east and strained past, and he stood there watching it go westward along the track and his train began to move, creeping eastward slow and feeling forward, and I watched it go and long as I could see him he was standing there, still and quiet, looking straight out along the back trail.

Well. I've taken you to where I was headed. It's only a hop now to those moccasins. I tried to tell the other boys about it the next day and likely boasted and strutted in the telling and they wouldn't believe me. Oh, they'd believe I saw the Indians all right. Had to. The telegraph operator backed my saying I was there. Even that I went aboard. But they wouldn't believe the rest. And because they wouldn't believe me I had to keep pounding it at them, telling it over and over. Expect I was getting to be mighty unpopular. But Jacob saved me even though I never saw him again. There was a day a bunch of us boys were playing some game or

172 other back of the telegraph shack and sudden we realized someone had come up from somewhere and was watching us. An Indian. Seemed to be just an ordinary everyday sort of tame Indian. But he was looking us over intent and careful and he picked me and came straight to me. He put out a hand, palm flat and down, and said something to me in his Indian talk and pointed off to the east and south and back again to me and reached inside the old blanket he had fastened around him with a belt and took out a dirty cloth-wrapped package and laid it at my feet and went away and faded out of sight around the shack. When I unrolled that package there were those moccasins.

Funny thing. I never wanted to go around telling my story to the other boys again. Didn't need to. Whether they believed or not wasn't important any more. I had those moccasins. In a way they made me one of Jacob's children. Remembering that has helped me sometimes in tough spots.

About the Author

Jack Warner Schaefer was born in Cleveland in 1907. After studying at Oberlin College and Columbia, he did educational work in the Connecticut prisons for seven years, and then turned to newspaper work. He achieved national fame in 1949 for *Shane*, his novel about an ex-gunman. The moving picture version of the book made Mr. Schaefer even more famous. "Jacob" comes from a recent collection of short stories called *The Plainsmen*. Mr. Schaefer currently lives in Santa Fe, New Mexico.

FOR DISCUSSION

Understanding the Story

1. "Jacob," another story of the West, deals with Indians and Indian wars.

   a. What are some of the usual TV and moving picture "western" features that are missing from this story?

   b. Why do you think these usual features are missing from this story?

2. The story does contain a description of the Nez Percé's conflict with the government soldiers: the origins, the way the fighting went, and the results. As you read this account, which side did you sympathize with? Why?

3. How did the boy's feelings about the Indians compare with yours? See if you can explain *all* the influences which made him feel as he did.

4. Why was the boy so surprised when he saw the actual Indians on the train? You, being older and wiser than the boy was then, should be able to explain why the Indians acted as they did on that train.

5. Jacob himself appears very briefly near the close of the story, in an incident that involves him with a soldier, a captain, and the boy. What did the boy learn from this incident?

Understanding the Theme

In "The Bishop's Silver" and "What Men Live By," you learned about the theme of a story—the underlying idea, the message, the particular truth which the author wants to convey to his reader. You learned that the theme is more than the plot; it arises out of the events of the story and the actions of the characters.

"Jacob" also has a theme, a theme of great importance in the world today. The questions that follow should help you to see what that theme is.

1. In the first part of the story, the narrator gives the facts, the truth, about the causes of the Indian wars. You will

find these facts in that part of the story that begins with the last paragraph on page 157. You will also find these facts in the description of the Nez Percé war.

a. What was the *truth* about the causes of the war?

b. What was the *truth* about the character of the Indians?

c. How much truth was there in the opinion of Indians that the boy got from his father and from his community?

d. What word can be used to describe a situation in which one group of people dislike or hate another group for reasons that are not based on the actual facts?

2. Because you are wiser than the boy in the story, you are aware of his errors in thinking about the Indians. However, the night that he visits the Indians on the train, he learns a great deal about himself and about the Indians. He learns this gradually. What does each of the statements below reveal about what he must have learned?

a. "And they [the Indians] weren't big and they weren't fierce at all. They were huddled figures on the coach seats . . . all dusty and tired and hunched together at the shoulders. . . ."

b. "They knew I was there. . . . But they wouldn't look at me. They were somehow off away in a place all their own and they weren't going to let me come near getting in there with them. . . ."

c. ". . . Jacob wasn't big or fierce. . . . He was short. . . . And his face was quiet and—well, the only word I can ever think of is peaceful. . . . And sudden I felt ashamed. . . ."

d. " 'There's fools of every color,' the captain said and Jacob's eyes brightened a little as if he understood. . . ."

e. "He [Jacob] was looking back along the iron trail that was taking him and his children away from a valley that would make a man want to put his feet firm on the earth and stretch tall and was taking them

to an unknown place where they could not be themselves any longer. . . ."

f. "It wasn't an Indian I was seeing there any more. It
was a man. . . . It was Mountain Elk . . . and he was
big, really big, and he was one meant to walk the
high places." (In what sense was Jacob "really big"?)

3. Why does the author begin and end with moccasins?
Rereading the last two sentences of the story will help
you answer this question.

4. How would you sum up the theme of this story, as it
applies not only to whites and Indians, but to others as
well? What specific problems in your community or your
state, or in our country or the world as a whole does
the theme of this story apply to?

VOCABULARY GROWTH

Using Word Parts to Build New Words

One way in which our language has grown is through
the building up of new words from old words. Your vocabulary can grow in the same way. One type of such "building up" is through the addition of certain suffixes (word
endings) to familiar words. Sometimes a slight change in
the spelling of the original word is necessary when a suffix
is added.

1. In this story, the author used a number of adjectives and
adverbs (words that describe) which consisted of a root
word and an added suffix. Below are some quotations
from the story which contain such words, along with
explanations which show how the words were formed.
The meaning of each suffix is given in parentheses. Notice how the addition of the suffix influenced the meaning of each word.

a. *"ceremonial* appearances": *ceremonial* = ceremony
+ al (pertaining to)

b. "they went *peaceable*": *peaceable* = peace + able
(able to, inclined to)

c. "time seemed to hang *motionless*": *motionless* =
motion + less (without)

d. "the *forgetful* government": *forgetful* = forget + ful
(full of)

e. "creeping *eastward*": *eastward* = east + ward (toward)

f. "*foolish* kids": *foolish* = fool + ish (like, having the
quality of)

g. "*dangerous* Indians": *dangerous* = danger + ous
(full of)

2. Below is a list of additional words with each of the above
suffixes. Check your dictionary for the meaning of each
word. How does the suffix influence the meaning?

fraternal   relentless   northward   glamorous
disputable bountiful   sheepish

Add two additional words of your own containing each
of the suffixes indicated.

FOR COMPOSITION

1. As a young child did you have any prejudices about a
group of people—a nationality, a religion, a social class,
a race? Explain what these ideas were, how you got
them, and what you think now of these ideas.

2. Which prejudices in your community or in our country
would you like to see eliminated? Explain what you
think should be done to eliminate one or more of them.

3. Perhaps you think there is too much talk about prejudice
going around today, and that we ought to let things
stay as they are. Explain why you feel this way.

TWO STORIES
ABOUT
SPORTS

Thicker Than Water

PAUL GALLICO

"Blood is thicker than water," the saying goes.
In this exciting story about prizefighting, a brother's
blood proves this statement to be surprisingly true.

THE OTHER day, I heard the story of how Tommy
White came back from a grave in the hard, white coral of
a South Pacific island where he sleeps under a wooden cross
on which his helmet hangs, rusting in the tropic rains, and
knocked out Tony Kid Marino in the seventh round at the
American Legion Stadium in our town.

Tommy White was a champion, but his kid brother Joey
was a dog. You often run across things like that. They were
both welterweights, and young Joey could box rings around
Tommy. He could have boxed those same circles around any
welterweight living if the geezer hadn't started to come out
in him after the first solid smack.

Tommy, on the other hand, had the heart of a lion. That is why he became a world's champion. That is why he enlisted the day after Pearl Harbor. That is why he walked into the machine-gun fire that was coming from a Japanese pillbox and murdering his company, and dropped a grenade into the slit, quietly and without fuss like a man posting a letter, before he died from being shot to pieces.

That sort of put the burden on Joey White and it seemed to be more of a load than he could lug. Doc Auer, who had managed Tommy and been more like a father to him, helped out all he could, but Doc wasn't exactly rich. Tommy had won his championship in the days when nobody got rich any more.

There was Mom White, and Phil, the youngest, and Anna, aged twelve, who had been living in a wheel chair ever since the hit-and-run driver had tossed her like a broken doll into the gutter. And, of course, there was Ellie, Tom's widow and their year-old baby.

Joey was a good kid. He couldn't help the yellow streak that came out in him in the ring. It often happens that way. Some boys don't like it. It was just that he would begin to blink and wince at the first solid smack, and then pretty soon he would be down, and you knew he wasn't bothering to get up.

Joey wasn't happy about his weakness. He tried to overcome it by going back into the ring, but each time he dogged it, it nearly drove him crazy, he felt so ashamed. There was the time he got pneumonia after he quit cold to Young Irish, and he hoped it would kill him. It nearly did, too, because he wouldn't fight the bug in him. Blood transfusion saved his life. Tommy, who was home on leave at the time, went to the hospital and acted as donor, though Joey never knew

180 about it. In the first place, hospitals don't tell, and, in the second, Tommy wasn't the kind who would mention such a trifle.

You hear a lot about fighters being no-goods and bums, but there are plenty of good kids in the game. The Whites were decent. When the news came about what had happened to Tommy in the Pacific, Joey went back to the ring. He might have got a job in a factory, but there were all the mouths to feed and the payments on the house. It wouldn't have been enough. And the ring was good for money now that there weren't too many classy boys around, and cards were hard to find. Joey had picked up a ruptured eardrum in one of his early fights and was 4-F.

Doc managed him, which was rough on Doc because he had loved Tommy like a son. Doc was a square shooter with a hook nose and tender hands that could soothe pain when he dressed damage in the corner. But he was a rough guy who couldn't stand ki-yi in his boys. What made it worse was that Doc knew Joey had it in him to be a bigger champion and a better fighter than Tommy ever was if he didn't curl up inside when the going got rough.

You would think after Tommy being killed the way he was, it would have given Joey the guts to go in there and pitch leather. The kid had loved his brother with a sort of doglike affection even though Tommy had always overshadowed him. But it didn't work out that way. In his first fight he quit to Ruby Schloss after being out in front five rounds and having Ruby on the floor. It was a good enough brawl so that Doc could get Joey another match, but when he folded to Arch Clement, who wasn't much more than 138 pounds, from a left hook to the chin that shouldn't have bothered a flyweight, it wasn't so good.

Four F, or no Four F, the fans want a fight when they pay their money, and you can't draw flies with a loser even in wartime. Besides, the ringworms were on to Joey. The promoters just said, "No, thanks," when Doc came around looking for a fight.

So the match with Tony Kid Marino was just sheer luck. "Soapy" Glassman, matchmaker for the American Legion Stadium, told Doc: "Lissen, if there was anybody around under fifty years old who could put his hands up, I wouldn't let a beagle like Joey into my club through the back door."

But there was nobody around, and Marino was a sensation. Discharged from the Army for some minor disability, he had swept through the South and the Middle West by virtue of a paralyzing left hook. He was headed for Madison Square Garden and the big dough. Glassman had to have an opponent in a hurry. Joey got the match but everybody knew he was to be the victim in it. It was also plainly labeled "last chance."

Doc said to Joey: "I seen Marino train at Flaherty's Gym. He don't know nothin'. A smart boxer could stab him all night and he wouldn't catch up. But he hits you with that left hook, and you need a room in a hospital. You got to stay away from him. And if you get hit a punch, you got to keep boxing."

Joey said, "I'll try, Doc. Honest, I will this time."

He always said that. He always meant it—until that first hard punch chunked home.

Doc said, "Yeah, I heard that before. If we could win this one, we go in the Garden instead of that bum. Ah, nuts! A guy can dream, can't he?"

Joey did try. He could box like a phantom. He was a tall, skinny boy with light hair and dark eyes and a pale, serious

182 face. His long arms and smooth shoulders were deceptive because they packed an awful wallop any time he stayed on the ground long enough to get set. But the night he fought Marino he wasn't staying in one place long enough to throw dynamite. He was trying his level best to do what Doc told him—stay away, stab, box and win.

There was a crowd of eight thousand packing the Legion Arena when they rang the bell for round one but, to a man, it was there to see Marino, the new kayo sensation, stiffen somebody, and the fact that Joey White was in there made it just that much more certain. Nobody was even interested when Joey gave as pretty a boxing show as you could want to see in that first round and jabbed Marino dizzy.

In fact, some wise guy started something by holding up one finger at the end of the round and shouting, "One!" That meant one round had gone by and Joey was still there. Pretty soon everybody in the arena took it up at the end of each round. It went on that way: "Two!" "Three!" "Four!"

Marino was muscled like a bulldog. He had short, black hair and dark skin, and he moved forward with a kind of dark sneer on his face as he tried to herd Joey into a corner where he could club his brains out.

Doc wasn't daring to breathe when round six came up, and Joey was still there and so far out ahead on points it wasn't even funny. He hadn't been hit yet. Four more rounds —then Madison Square Garden, the big dough, a shot at the championship, security for Tommy's family. In and out went Joey—feint and stab, jab and step away, jab and circle, pop-pop-pop, three left hands in a row.

So then it happened just before the end of the sixth. The ropes on the south side of the ring had got slack and didn't have the snap-back Joey expected when he came off them, which caused him to be sufficiently slow for Marino's hook to catch him. It hit Joey on the shoulder and knocked him halfway across the ring.

Now, nobody ever got knocked out with a punch to the arm. But it was all over. Everybody knew it. Everybody saw the look come into Joey's eyes, the curl to his mouth and the cringe to his shoulders. It was the promise of things to come conveyed by the punch, that did it. The swarthy Marino leaped after Joey to find a lethal spot, but the bell rang, ending the round.

The crowd stood up, held up six fingers and yelled, "Six!" and the wag who had started it shouted, "Seventh and last coming up!" and everybody howled with laughter

Joey went to his corner and sat down, but Doc, who was usually in the ring before the echoes of the bell had died away, cotton swabs sticking out of his mouth, sponge in hand, ready to loosen trunks and administer relief and attention, remained outside the ropes. He didn't so much as touch Joey. He just leaned down with his head through the space between the top and second strand, and talked out of the side of his mouth into Joey's ear.

He said, "Ya bum! You going to quit in the next round, ain't you?"

Joey moved on the stool and touched his shoulder. "My arm. It's numb."

Doc went right on talking quietly out of the side of his mouth as though he were giving advice: "Makin' out to quit and you ain't even been hurt yet. You got the fight won and you're gonna go out there and lay down, ain't you?"

Joey didn't say anything any more but licked his lips and shuffled his feet in the resin and tried to hide his eyes so nobody would see the fear that was in them.

Doc said, "I ought to bust the bottle over your head. You, with the blood of a champion in your veins, makin' to go out there and lay down like a dog."

Joey turned and looked at Doc, and his lips moved. Under the hubbub he said, "What are you talking about?"

"What I said. A guy you ain't even fit to think about. You got his blood in you. He give it to you when you was sick in the hospital and had to have a blood infusion.

"I . . . I got Tommy's blood?"

The ten-second buzzer squawked.

Doc said, "Yeah. You got it, only it dried up when it come to your chicken heart. Okay, bum, go on out there and take the dive." Then he quietly climbed down the ring steps. The bell rang for the seventh round.

Everything happened then as expected. Joey came out with his hands held too low and he seemed to be trembling. Marino ran over and swept a clublike left to the side of his head, and Joey went down as everybody knew he would.

Only thereafter he did what no one expected or had ever seen him do before. He rolled over and got on one knee, shaking his head a little, and listened to the count until it got to eight. Then he got up.

His head was singing, but his heart was singing louder. Tommy's blood! His brother's blood, the blood of one of the gamest champions in the world, coursing through his veins. A part of Tommy's life was alive inside of him. . . .

The referee finished wiping the resin from his gloves and stepped aside. Marino shuffled over, his left cocked. Joey dropped his hands still lower and stuck out his chin. The stocky little Italian accepted the invitation and hit it with all his power, knocking Joey back into the ropes.

But he didn't go down. Marino followed up, pumping left and right to Joey's head, rocking him from side to side.

The crowd was screaming and above the roar someone was shouting, "Cover up! Cover up, you fool!"

Cover up for what? This bum? He couldn't hit hard enough to knock out a man with a champion's blood in his veins. Joey seemed to feel his blood stream like fire all through his body. He could take it, take it, take it now, he could sop it up, punch after punch, and not go down, never again go down as long as in his heart there beat and pulsed the warm life of his brother.

Marino fell back wheezing and gasping for air and strength to carry on the assault. Joey laughed and came off the ropes. Marino had punched himself out, had he? That was how Tommy used to get them.

Joey came down off his toes. His stance changed abruptly, hands at belt level, but nearer to his body. He edged close to Marino and chugged two shot blows into his middle, whipping the punches with body leverage, and the crowd roared to its feet. Men sitting in the back rows swore it was as though they were seeing Tommy White again.

Marino grunted, turned ashen and retreated. Strength coursed like hot wine through Joey's limbs. He pressed forward, anchored to the canvas floor like a sturdy tree and raised his sights. The short, sharp, murderous punches whipped to Marino's swarthy jaw. Through the smoky air the gloves flew—punch, punch, punch!

When there was nothing more in front of him to punch, Joey leaned from a neutral corner and bawled at the body on the canvas as the referee's arm rose and fell, "Get up.... Get up and fight! I ain't finished yet."

Then somehow he was in Doc's arms. Doc was kissing him and there were tears on Doc's face and he was crying, "Tommy ... Tommy ... Joey boy.... It was just like Tommy

186 was alive again. Joey, baby, there ain't nothing goin' to stop you now...."

About the Author

Paul Gallico, born in New York in 1897, has always been interested in sports, as both a participant and an observer. He was captain of the crew at Columbia College. And he has tried over thirty other sports because of his desire to "know how it feels" to be an active part of them. Mr. Gallico has even persuaded sports stars to play against him. Once he boxed with Jack Dempsey and was kayoed in one minute and twenty-three seconds. After this boxing bout Mr. Gallico said, "I knew all there was to know about being hit."

Mr. Gallico eventually became the highest paid sports writer in the newspaper world when he was sports columnist for the New York *Daily News*. Later he gave up journalism for fiction, publishing many short stories and several novels.

You probably observed how closely familiar with the world of boxing Paul Gallico is when you read "Thicker Than Water."

FOR DISCUSSION

Understanding the Story

1. In this story, Joey is contrasted with his older brother, Tommy. What differences were there between them?

2. Did the author want you to be sympathetic with Joey in the first part of the story, or did he want you to be

against him? What were you told about him that made **187** you feel as you did?

3. Why did Doc speak so harshly to Joey between rounds six and seven? Was he "letting off steam" or did he have another purpose?

4. What caused the change in Joey that enabled him to win?

5. The first sentence of the story tells us that Tommy White (dead on the field of battle) "came back...and knocked out Tony Kid Marino." In what sense was this true?

Understanding the Art of the Writer

1. What did you notice about the language of the person who is telling the story? Why did Mr. Gallico, the author, tell the story in this way?

2. Reread the paragraph on page 185, beginning "Marino grunted, turned ashen. . . ." How did the author make the reader feel as though he were right there in a ringside seat? Pick out words and phrases that had this effect, and explain why they were so effective.

(Further discussion of "Thicker Than Water" is provided in the questions which follow the next story, "Independence Day.")

VOCABULARY GROWTH

Using Context to Unlock Word Meanings

This story contains many expressions which you may never find in an ordinary dictionary. They are words which prizefighters and others who are associated with professional boxing use among themselves.

Such words, used by those in a certain occupation, are called the *jargon* of that profession.

You can probably guess what these words mean from the context in which they appear. Find the part

1. "Tommy White was a champion, but his kid brother Joey was a *dog*." (page 178)

2. "He could have boxed those same circles around any welterweight living if the *geezer* hadn't started to come out in him after the first solid smack." (page 178)

3. "He tried to overcome it by going back into the ring, but each time he *dogged it....*" (page 179)

4. "But he was a rough guy who couldn't stand *ki-yi* in his boys." (page 180)

5. "You would think . . . it would have given Joey the *guts* to go in there and *pitch leather*." (page 180)

6. ". . . but when he *folded* to Arch Clement . . . it wasn't so good." (page 180)

7. " 'Lissen, if there was anybody around under fifty years old who could put his hands up, I wouldn't let a *beagle* like Joey into my club through the back door.' " (page 181)

8. " 'Okay, bum, go on out there and *take the dive*.' " (page 184)

FOR COMPOSITION

1. Did you notice how Paul Gallico made the last part of the story exciting by using specific, vivid words and comparisons? Try to describe a real or imaginary exciting event, using the same technique.

2. Sometimes a story seems natural and real just because it is told in language that isn't cultured or formal. It is told in the kind of language which a character in the story would naturally use.

Young people today have their own *jargon*, their own vocabulary which may not be that of their parents or teachers. "Jive" talk and "hip" talk are examples of such language; there are probably other examples among **189** your friends.

Try writing about some incident that happened to you or your friends, using some of the natural language that is spoken in your group.

3. A very large proportion of professional athletes today in such sports as boxing, baseball, basketball, and football are members of minority groups, such as blacks and Spanish-Americans. Write a composition in which you explain why you think this has happened.

Independence Day

A. B. GUTHRIE, JR.

Everyone was out to have a grand time on this
Independence Day, watching a man who deserved
it being beaten in the boxing ring. Among the
spectators, only Charlie didn't have a good time.
Was something wrong with him, or with the others?

It was July 4, 1920, and Charlie Bostwick was
seventeen years old when Bill the Butch fought the Fairfax
Soldier. It was a big day in Moon Dance because everybody
wanted so to see Bill beaten.

Bill was a young German who had drifted into town
from somewhere and had got a job at Nick's Meat Market,
where he swept and scrubbed and made deliveries and
helped with the butchering at the slaughterhouse that made
a stink in the river woods two miles south of town. Nick
didn't let him wait on trade. "He dun't spik English so good,
y'knaw, and dun't know meat yet needer," Nick explained.
"He t'ink too good of himself already, yah, but he fine vorker,
you bet."

190

Nick would say things like that even when Bill the Butch was around, but they didn't seem to bother Bill at all. When he had a chance, he still talked about prize fighting and told what a fighter he was. He was with a bunch of Charlie's high school classmates when Charlie first saw him, at the side door of the butcher shop. "I love fight," he said, looking at the boys. His eyes were bright and blue as blue glass, his face square and simple. "Fight, dat fun for real man. Hah, I vish I be v'ere good men vas." He made a couple of determined passes at the air. "I show 'em. I hit strong, like a kick." He looked down at his thick, stubby-fingered hands and closed them into fists and brought the fists up where he could see them close. "Boomp!" he said, "boomp!" making little jabs with one of them.

Charlie couldn't hold back the question, "What're you doing around here, if you're so good?"

Bill said, "Hah! I take two of you, t'ree, and boomp, boomp, boomp, like dat." His hands came back to his sides, and his fists opened after the knockouts.

In a way his words were a dare, and the boys looked at him, then at one another, and back to him, and Charlie found himself scuffing his shoes on the sidewalk. And in a way they weren't a dare, either, but, what was worse, a kind of insult, said as if Bill was too good a man to bother with the likes of them. It was as if Bill hadn't been talking to them, as if, instead of seeing them, he saw a prize ring over their heads and himself in it and people yelling for him. In the long afternoon sunlight his eyes gleamed.

Bill made another pass at the air, picked up the broom he had been sweeping the walk with and let himself in the shop, his chest swelled out and his eyes still shining and distant.

Afterward George Jackson said, "Jeez, Charlie!"

Charlie didn't say anything for a while. He walked along, thinking and feeling sore inside. "Someone ought to take a poke at him," he said then, as much to himself as to George.

"You want to?"

"Think I'm scared to?"

"You got better sense, I hope. You could lick him in English or geometry, is all, like you lick me, but he would beat you all to hell with one hand tied behind him."

"Stuck on himself."

"Nothing you can do."

Charlie said, "He'll get his some day."

The day seemed a long time coming. There were men in town who maybe could have whipped Bill, but they didn't try. Charlie didn't know the reason, unless it was that Bill was so sure of himself. Or maybe it was that he never talked to a person as if he figured that person could be a match for him, or even figured that the person could see himself as one. Bill's men were all far-off, mighty fighters like you read about in the newspapers. Burt Upham, who was a little old and always smelled of whisky, growled around about teaching a young pup a lesson, but he never did, though he was big and powerful and had been in lots of fights. And the men just back from the war talked mean but didn't act. "Damn squarehead," they called Bill. "He don't know Germany lost the war. Like all them Heinies he thinks he's number one."

While they cussed him, Bill just went on talking and making passes at the air going to and from the delivery truck, and after a while it got to be a kind of sour sport just to egg him on. When he came into Gorham's Pool Hall at night, someone was sure to ask about his condition or to ask him to show his knock-'em-dead punch, and a little crowd would gather around him and smile at one another out of the corners of their mouths while Bill talked or shadow-boxed. Like everybody else Charlie wished someone would take him down a peg.

It was the men back from the war and the new organization called the American Legion that finally set out to do it. Charlie heard about the plan from George. "The fight's gonna be the Fourth," George announced. "They got a ex-soldier from Fairfax and, boy, is he good! He was a champ in the army. That's what they say."

"Who is he? What kind of a champ?"

"I forgit. All I know is he's a cinch, and Mr. Bill the Brag sure as hell will count stars."

Charlie felt an eager gnawing in his chest. He said, "Gee!" and then said it again. "It'll be almost like the war over again."

"Just what I was thinking."

"Le's see what Bill says now!"

Bill wasn't in the shop, but came driving up after a while in the truck.

Charlie said, "Hear you got a real fight on your hands, Bill?"

"Yah."

"Gonna win?"

"Sure I vin."

"Sure?"

"I knock 'im out qvick."

George said, "It's a champ you're fightin', you know."

"I hope he stand oop for little v'ile so people get some-ding for money. You vait. You see how good dis Vilhelm iss." His feet did a little dance, and his left stabbed at the air and his right came over. He went on into the shop.

The town was crowded on the Fourth. The Legion had

194 arranged for a parade and a patriotic speaking and for fire-works at night, but it was the fight that brought people in. The Legion had built a high, solid-board fence around a vacant lot and had set up a ring in it. Charlie and George went in at two o'clock, a half hour before time for the fight, so as to be sure to get places close to the ring. There were no seats inside; everybody had to stand; but the ring had been raised to make seeing easier, and, as the lot filled up, those in back stood on boxes or clung to the fence while standing on the runners at the bottom of it.

Bill the Butch came to the ring first. He had on a dirty old bathrobe and, underneath it, a pair of faded purple trunks. He walked with his head up. He didn't look scared but calm and sure, as if he was as good as anybody and probably better. Bill grabbed a rope and lifted himself easily into the ring. Burt Upham, his second, had a harder time getting up. When he was in his corner he turned around, away from Bill, and gave the crowd a big wink. People laughed because they knew Upham wanted Bill licked as much as anyone.

Bill took off his robe and began squatting up and down while he held on to the ropes. To Charlie he didn't look exactly muscular but only big and heavy and even a little bit fat. His body was white like a grub's, and like a grub's it struck you as something you wouldn't want to feel.

Charlie heard cheers and saw the Fairfax Soldier elbow-ing through the crowd toward the other corner. When he was on the platform Charlie saw he was a tall, lean man, roped with long muscles. The skin of his face was dark and tight-drawn, his eyes sharp and wary. Under the small nose, his mouth made a tight line. He began flexing himself, too. The pair of them came to the center of the ring, looked at each other's gloves, heard Referee Sam King say something, shook hands quickly and went to their corners. George breathed, "Oh, boy!" into Charlie's ear.

The bell rang. Bill the Butch ran from his corner, head down, like a tackler. He swung overhand, left first, then the right—two long, fierce blows backed by the weight of his running body. The right smashed square in the Soldier's face. The Soldier's head snapped back. He hunched forward afterwards with his gloves before his face and sidled around. When he straightened, Bill charged again. And again it was the overhand one-two, and again the Soldier's head snapped. A trickle of blood started from his nose. Charlie half expected to see fear in his eyes, but all he saw, when the Soldier faced around, was the sure, sharp wariness of an animal.

Bill ran across the ring, flung left and right, and landed again. The Soldier faltered a little at the knees. He clung to Bill, so that the referee had to part them. The Soldier staggered, backing off.

Charlie heard breathing around him, all breaths going into one great, hungry breathing, with yells locked quiet in the throats except now and then for a strained, high cry.

The bell sounded as Bill set himself for another charge. Charlie heard someone say, "Maybe we'll have to ride the son-of-a-gun out of town on a rail after all." There was a frown on Burt Upham's face. He made a swipe at Bill's face and chest with a towel. Bill's chest rose and fell, big as a bellows, while he leaned back on his stool. There wasn't even a flush on his white grub's body. In the other corner Terry Frimmer was sloshing wet towels on the Soldier's face and chest and standing back afterwards and fanning him. The Soldier didn't take his eyes off Bill. He studied him steadily, as if looking for the weak spot. The water and towels had stopped the trickle of blood.

Bill was on his feet before the bell rang. When it did, he went into his hard, lumbering run and threw his pair of punches. A roar went up on all sides of Charlie, the great, hungry roar that had been locked in the throats, for as Bill struck with his left and right the Fairfax Soldier slipped to one side and brought an uppercut from his knees. The smash of it was like the sound of a bat against a bag of grain. The blow jerked Bill straight. It bewildered him. For an instant he stood with his guard down and took two hard licks to the body before he got backed up and so in position to charge again. Out of the roar Charlie could hear single cries now. "Kill him, Soldier!" "Kill the squarehead!" Bill didn't land one good blow in the rest of the round, and once more he ran into that smashing uppercut.

When he came back to his corner, his face seemed out of focus, the upper lip swollen big under the nose and the nose looking flattened and the bright blue eyes clouded. There were angry blotches on his belly, standing red against the white.

But at the start of the third round he jumped up and charged. It was as if he didn't know any better. It was as if he didn't know anything but the charge and the one-two, and then the uppercut landing in his face and the blood flowing from him now and smearing his face and splashing down on the bulge of his belly. "Bleeds easy, the damn butcher!" "Put him away, Soldier!" "Yowee!" The charge, the one-two, the uppercut, the Soldier fighting relaxed and easy and his tight mouth loose in a smile and his sharp eyes smiling, too, and the white grub gory, and people hoarse with yelling.

Bill went down at the start of the fourth round. He had charged and struck wildly and met the uppercut and, dazed, had fallen before a straight right. He scrambled up fast, as if embarrassed, as if ashamed of himself, as if caught publicly in something bad as sin. He wobbled into his lunge. It was all he knew, the one part of fighting, the single, sorry trick.

Charlie couldn't make himself yell. He felt a little sick. He tried to shake away a feeling of shame, shame for himself and all the whoopers baying their glad whoops. They weren't men enough for Bill themselves, and so they had gone out meanly and got themselves a man, and now you'd think that each of them was whipping Bill himself.

Bill went down, he wavered to his feet, he stumbled ahead, always ahead, making his fists poke out, falling again and making himself rise from his shame.

The final blow slammed Bill on his back. His body made a jerk or two, as if his very will would force it through un- consciousness, and then lay still. The referee counted to ten. Burt Upham climbed into the ring with a pail of water. He was grinning, like everybody else. Over the ropes he said, "There, by God, is a good German." Some men were still whooping, and some were pounding others on the back. A crowd had the Fairfax Soldier in their arms, carrying him overhead.

Charlie couldn't take his eyes off Bill, lying white-and- red, lying in shame, and all his bull's courage dead with him and all his pride.

"Jeez!" George said into his ear. "It was swell, wasn't it?"

Charlie didn't answer.

George hit him on the back. "Swell, huh?"

Charlie didn't quite meet George's eyes. "Yeah, I guess so."

"You guess so!"

"Let's get out of here."

Walking away, through men still hurrahing and passing Prohibition flasks, now, to celebrate, Charlie kept seeing Bill the Butch, beaten and abased and lying like naked while eyes looked on and mouths jeered.

George asked, "You say something?"

"I was just wondering."

"About what?"

"Things."

"Like what?"

"Nothing."

"You act like you wanted Bill to win!"

"I didn't say that."

"Bill had it coming."

"I said I was just wondering."

"You know he had it coming."

"I know he had it coming, damn it! I didn't say he didn't have it coming."

"O.K. then. Let's shoot one game."

"I got to get home."

"Meet me at the pool hall after supper, and we'll go to the fireworks."

"All right."

Charlie walked home, feeling heavy inside and downcast, as if he'd done something wrong. He sat down under the cottonwood tree in the front yard and by and by got out his knife and picked at the turf with it, letting the fight run in his mind's eye and the shouts sound again in his ears while the sun slid behind the house and day cooled off toward evening. After a while his mother called him in to eat.

By the time supper was over he knew what he wanted to do. He wanted to see Bill. He had to talk to Bill.

Bill lived in Nick's house. It was part of his pay, living

there was, and maybe it was as good or better than what he had known before, though the room was in the basement and a person got to it by lifting a door and walking down concrete steps that gritted under the feet with the ashes that had been spilled on the way up.

Charlie walked past the furnace to the corner and knocked at the plank door and heard a voice say something. He turned the slick, black knob and stepped in. Bill stood in the middle of the room, holding a wet towel to one side of his face. It flashed into Charlie's mind that the treatment hadn't done much good, no matter how long Bill had been at it. He could see the lips were thick on the side not covered by the towel, and one eye was puffed and purpling so that the gaze out of it seemed small and pointed. He thought the face looked lonesome. There was an iron bed in the room, where Bill had been lying, and a straight-backed chair and a bare lighted bulb hanging from the ceiling and a chiffonier with a basin of water on it and a cracked mirror over it.

Charlie said the words that came to his mouth. He said, "I'm sorry, Bill," and the saying made him feel better. It was as if he had cleansed himself and somehow cleansed the whoopers, too. "You put up a good fight."

Bill said, "You vait!"

"You fought fine."

"Nodder time, I kill 'im. He vas lucky, iss all."

Bill took the towel from his cheek and stuck out his square, swollen face. "I vas soft. No one to spar mit. No place. I get fixed next time. No-good fighter, dot soldier. Ah-h!"

"He fought all right."

"Ah-h! No-good fighter. Already I t'ink how to do it. I train every day. I be ready. I better man, you bet."

"It's all over."

"You iss only friend for me. Maybe I teach you to fight.

200 You can spar mit me, yah. I let you spar mit Vilhelm." The blue eyes waited for a yes.

Charlie said, "I don't guess so. I guess I wouldn't want to do that." He waited to see what Bill would do, making himself hold the blue eyes with his own, making himself hold the thickened face. He turned then and walked from the room, across the darkening basement and up the gritty steps.

For a minute, as he raised his hand to lift the outside door, he hesitated, wondering who might see him come out. Then he pushed the door open and stepped up and out and straightened himself and let the door fall behind him.

There was no one to see him, but up the street, through shadows blurring out toward dusk, he caught sight of George, headed, he guessed, for the pool hall. He found himself hurrying, feeling good of a sudden, feeling released, wanting to shout and run and catch up and throw his arm across George's shoulders and walk with him to the friendly rightness of the pool hall and the later fireworks.

Then he heard the shout again, the great shout breaking from its strangle, and he saw the glad, hungry eyes and the working mouths and one man down who had it coming, and his step slowed and came to a stop at a corner that George just had crossed. After a while he turned half around and began lagging down the street, away from George and the hall and the rockets that would sprinkle sparks against the dark.

About the Author

Almost from the day of his birth in 1901, A. B. Guthrie, Jr. grew up with a passionate interest in the West and its history. He got it from his father, a teacher in Montana. After college graduation Mr. Guthrie became a reporter and newspaper editor. In 201 1944 he won a newspaper fellowship to Harvard, and under the influence of one of his professors began to write a novel, *The Big Sky*, which proved to be a best seller. A later novel, *The Way West*, won the Pulitzer Prize in 1949.

Because he loves the outdoors, Mr. Guthrie today lives again in Montana, the probable setting for "Independence Day." In 1965 he published his autobiography, *The Blue Hen's Chick*.

FOR DISCUSSION

Understanding the Story

1. What were the reasons why everyone disliked Bill the Butch? Did you feel the same way or differently?

2. Reread the part of the story that describes the actual fight and its result. Pick out the sentences which show the feelings of the crowd as Bill the Butch was being beaten by the Fairfax Soldier. How would you summarize the feelings and the behavior of the crowd?

3. Compare Charlie's feelings with those of the crowd. What made him feel as he did?

4. Charlie says to Bill after the fight: " 'I'm sorry, Bill.' " What do you suppose he was really sorry about?

5. How do you explain Charlie's feelings toward Bill after the fight? Did he like him then? Did he dislike him? Or were his feelings mixed and complicated?

In answering this question, you should consider several things in the story: Charlie's character, Bill's behavior during the fight, the crowd's behavior, Bill's behavior after the fight, and the conditions in which Bill seemed to be living in that town.

6. a. Why did Charlie feel "good of a sudden" after his visit to Bill?

b. How do you explain the last two sentences in the story?

Understanding the Theme

1. Reread the paragraph on page 194, beginning "Charlie couldn't make himself yell." The paragraph tells us that Charlie was ashamed, for himself and the crowd. Why was he ashamed?

2. Do you think Charlie was right or wrong in being ashamed? Give reasons.

3. When, in any work of literature, the truth about a situation is the opposite of what seems to be true, we say there is irony in that situation.

a. Do you see any irony in the title "Independence Day"? How much "independence" did the people show on this Fourth of July?

b. For one person in the story, this day *was* Independence Day. For whom? Why?

4. Do you remember the boys who played ball in "The New Kid"? If Charlie had been one of those boys, how might the story have been different?

5. How would you sum up the theme of "Independence Day"?

Comparing Two Stories

"Thicker Than Water" and "Independence Day" both deal with fighters in the boxing ring. It may be interesting to compare them in certain respects.

1. In both stories an important change takes place in the main character. In which story is the change more natural, more realistic, more believable? Explain your answer, referring to both stories.

2. Which story gave you more to think about? Why?

3. In which story does human nature seem to be more simple and uncomplicated? In which story does human nature appear to be less simple, more complicated? Prove your answer.

   Which type of story, the first or the second, do you think represents more accurately the truth about human nature? Explain your answer.

4. Which of the stories is more likely to influence you in your own behavior as you grow older? Why?

VOCABULARY GROWTH

Appreciating the Author's Use of Comparisons

Often, when a writer wants to express an idea or a picture especially strongly or vividly, he does so by comparisons. Such comparisons are called *figures of speech.*

Each of the five sentences below contains a figure of speech. In each case, explain what effect or picture you get from this figure of speech; explain also why the comparison is appropriate or fitting for the writer's purpose. In each sentence, one key word is italicized. Look that word up in the dictionary if you are not sure of its meaning.

1. "His [Bill's] body was white like a *grub's,* and like a grub's it struck you as something you wouldn't want to feel."

2. "... Charlie saw he [the Fairfax Soldier] was a tall, lean man, *roped* with long muscles."

3. "Charlie half expected to see fear in his eyes, but all he saw, when the Soldier faced around, was the sure, sharp *wariness* of an animal."

4. "Bill's chest rose and fell, big as a *bellows...*"

5. "He [Charlie] tried to shake away a feeling of shame, shame for himself and all the whoopers *baying* their glad whoops."

FOR COMPOSITION

1. Have you ever known an occasion when a crowd acted in a way you didn't like? Tell what happened, and explain why you objected to the crowd's behavior.

2. It is said that no one is completely bad; that if we really know enough about even the worst person, we will find reason to sympathize with him.

   Do you think this can be true? Write a composition in which you give your opinion. If you can, support your opinion by using someone you have known as an example.

3. Many people think boxing should be abolished as a sport. Explain why you agree or disagree with this view.

STORIES
ABOUT
YOUNG PEOPLE

Enemy Territory

WILLIAM MELVIN KELLEY

It's hard to say when a child begins to mature, to
learn what an adult needs to know. Tommy, in this
story, was only six years old, a black child whose
parents had brought him up to be peaceful and
gentle. When he was sent on an errand and was
stopped by a gang of boys, he retreated. But his
grandmother, much to his surprise, didn't like what
she saw. When she told him the story of Pablo, his
Cuban grandfather, who had also been peaceful
and gentle, Tommy went on his errand again
with a new point of view.

I PEERED over a rotting tree stump and saw him moving, without a helmet, in the bushes. I got his forehead in my sights, squeezed the trigger, and imagined I saw the bullet puncture his head and blood trickle out. "I got you, Jerome. I got you!"

"Awh, you did not."

"I got you; you're dead."

I must have sounded very definite because he compromised. "You only wounded me."

"Tommy? Tommy! Come here." Her voice came from high above me.

I scrambled to my knees. "What, Ma?" She was on the porch of our house, next to the vacant lot where we were playing.

"Come here a minute, dear. I want you to do something for me." She was wearing a yellow dress. The porch was red brick.

I hopped up and ran to the foot of our steps. She came to the top. "Mister Bixby left his hat."

As I had waited in ambush for Jerome, I had seen Mister Bixby climb and, an hour later, chug down the steps. He was one of my father's poker playing friends. It was only after she mentioned it that I remembered Mister Bixby had been wearing, when he arrived, a white, wide-brimmed panama hat with a black band.

Entering my parents' room on the second floor, I saw it on their bed. My mother picked it up. "Walk it around to his house. Now walk, I say. Don't run because you'll probably drop it and ruin it." It was so white a speck of dirt would have shone like a black star in a white sky. "So walk! Let me see your hands."

I extended them palms up and she immediately sent me to the bathroom to wash. Then she gave me the hat. I did not

208 really grip it, rather, with my finger in the crown, I balanced it, as if about to twirl it.

When I stepped onto the porch again, I saw them playing on their corner—Valentine's Gang. Well, in this day of street gangs organized like armies, I cannot rightly call Joey Valentine, who was eight, and his acquaintances, who ranged in age from five to seven, a gang. It was simply that they lived on the next block, and since my friends and I were just at the age when we were allowed to cross the street, but were not yet used to this new freedom, we still stood on opposite sides of the asphalt strip that divided us and called each other names. It was not until I got onto the porch that I realized, with a sense of dread that only a six-year-old can conjure up, that Mister Bixby lived one block beyond Valentine's Territory.

Still, with faith that the adult nature of my mission would give me unmolested passage, I approached the corner, which was guarded by a red fire alarm box, looked both ways for the cars that seldom came, and, swallowing, began to cross over.

They were playing with toy soldiers and tin tanks in the border of dry yellow dirt that separated the flagstones from the gutter. I was in the middle of the street when they first realized I was invading; they were shocked. At the time, I can remember thinking they must have been awed that I should have the unequaled courage to cross into their territory. But looking back, I realize it probably had little to do with me. It was the hat, a white panama hat. A more natural target for abuse has never existed.

I was two steps from the curb when Joey Valentine moved into my path. "Hey, what you got?"

Since he was obviously asking the question to show off, I bit my lips and did not answer. I saw myself as one of my radio heroes resisting Japanese interrogation. I was aloof.

However, the white panama hat was not at all aloof. Before I knew it, Joey Valentine reached out a mud-caked hand and knocked the hat off my finger to a resounding chorus of cheers and laughter.

I scooped up the hat before any of them, retreated at a run across the street, and stopped beside the red alarm box. Wanting to save some small amount of my dignity, I screamed at them: "I'll get you guys! I'll get you. I'm not really an American. I'm an African and Africans are friends of the Japs and I'll get them to *bomb your house!*"

But even as I ranted at them, I could see I was doing so in vain. Across the way, Valentine's Gang lounged with the calm of movie Marines listening to Japanese propaganda on the radio. I turned toward my house, inspecting the hat for smudges. There were none; it was as blinding white as ever. Already I felt tears inching down my cheeks.

Not until I was halfway up the porch steps did I see my grandmother sitting in her red iron chair. But before I could say anything, before I could appeal for understanding and comfort, she lifted herself out of the chair and disappeared into the house. She had seen it all—I knew that—and she was too ashamed of me to face me.

Suddenly, she was coming back, holding a broom handle. She had never before lifted a hand to me, but in my state, I felt sure that many things would change. I closed my eyes and waited.

Instead of the crunch of hard wood on bone, I heard her chair creak. I opened my eyes and found the end of the broom handle under my nose.

"You know if you don't go back and deliver that hat, you'll feel pretty bad tonight."

I nodded.

"Well, take this. We don't like you fighting. But sometimes you have to. So now you march down there and tell those boys if they don't let you alone, you'll have to hit them with this. Here." She pushed the broom handle at me.

I took it, but was not very happy about it. I studied her; she looked the same, her white hair bunned at her neck, her blue eyes large behind glasses, her skin the color of unvarnished wood. But something inside must have changed for her actually to tell me to hit someone. I had been in fights, fits and starts of temper that burned out in a second. But to walk deliberately down to the corner, threaten someone and hit him if he did not move aside, this was completely different, and, as my parents and grandmother had raised me, downright evil. She must have realized what I was thinking.

"You know who Teddy Roosevelt was?"

I nodded.

"Well, he once said: *Speak softly and carry a big stick; you will go far.*"

I understood her, but to do something like this was still alien to my nature. I held back.

"Come on." She stood abruptly and took my hand. We went into the house, down the hall, and into her bedroom. "I have to see to the mulatto rice. You sit on my bed and look at the picture on the wall." She went on to the kitchen. I was still holding the broom handle and now put it down across the bed, and climbed up beside it, surrounded by her room, an old woman's room with its fifty years of perfume, powder, and sweet soap. I felt a long way from the corner and Valentine's Gang.

There were three pictures on the wall and I was not certain which she wanted me to study. The smallest was of my granduncle Wilfred, who lived on Long Island and came to

Thanksgiving dinner. The largest was of Jesus, the fingers of His right hand crossed and held up, His left hand baring His chest in the middle of which was His heart, red and dripping blood. In the cool darkness of the room, He looked at me with gentle eyes, a slight smile on His lips. The third was my grandmother's husband, who had died so long before that I had never known him and had no feeling for him as my grandfather. He was light, like my grandmother, but more like some of the short, sallow Italian men who lived on the block. His black hair was parted in the middle. He wore a big mustache which hid his mouth. His jaw was square and dimpled. With black eyes, he seemed to look at something just above my head.

"Well, all right now." My grandmother came in, sweating from standing over the stove, and sat in a small arm chair beside the bed. "Did you look at the picture?"

"I didn't know which one." I looked at Jesus again.

"No, not Him this time. This one." She indicated her husband. "I meant him."

Now Pablo [Cortés,] your grandfather—she started—was just like you, as gentle as a milkweed flower settling into honey, and as friendly as ninety-seven puppy-dogs. He was from Cuba, which is an island in the Atlantic Ocean.

He was so kind that he'd meet every boat coming in from Cuba and talk to all of the people getting off, and if he found that one of them didn't have a place to stay, and no money for food, he'd bring him home. He'd lead his new friend into the kitchen and say: "Jennie, this is a countryman. He got no place to sleep, and he's hungry." And I'd sigh and say: "All right. Dinner'll be ready in ten minutes." They'd go into the living room and sing and roll cigars.

That's what he did for a living, roll cigars, working at home. The leaves were spread out all over the floor like a rug and I never did like cigars because I know somebody's been walking all over the leaves, sometimes in barefeet like your mother did when she was a little girl.

Pablo was so friendly he gave a party every day while I was at work. I'd come home and open the door and the cigar smoke would tumble out and through the haze I would see twenty drunken Cubans, most with guitars, others rolling cigars, and all of them howling songs.

So now fifty years ago, I'd come from down South to stay with my brother Wilfred, and I was so dumb that the first time I saw snow I thought somebody upstairs'd broken open a pillow out the window. So my brother Wilfred had to explain a lot of things to me. And the first thing was about the neighborhoods. In those days, New York was all split up into neighborhoods. The Italians lived in one neighborhood, and the Polish in another, and the Negroes and Cubans some place else. After Pablo and I got married, we lived with the Negroes. And if you walked two blocks one way, you'd come to the Irish neighborhood, and if you were smart, you'd turn around and come back because if the Irish caught you, they'd do something terrible to you.

I don't know if Pablo knew this or not, or if he just thought he was so friendly that everybody would just naturally be friendly right back. But one day he went for a walk. He got over into the Irish neighborhood and got a little thirsty—which he did pretty often—so he went into an Irish bar and asked for a drink. I guess they thought he was new in this country because the bartender gave him his drink. So Pablo, smiling all the time, and waiting for them to smile back, stood there in that Irish bar and drank slow. When he was finished

the bartender took the glass and instead of washing it, he
smashed it down on the floor and stepped on it and crushed
the pieces under his heel. What he meant was that it was
pretty bad to be a Cuban and no Irishman would want to
touch a glass a Cuban had drunk from.

I don't know if Pablo knew that either. He asked for another drink. And he got it. And after he finished this one, the
bartender smashed it in the sink and glared at him.

Pablo was still thirsty and ordered again.

The bartender came and stood in front of him. He was a
big man, with a face as red as watermelon. "Say, buddy,
can't you take a hint?"

Pablo smiled. "What hint?"

The bartender was getting pretty mad. "Why you think
I'm breaking them glasses?"

"I thought you like to break glasses. You must got a high
bill on glasses."

The bartender got an axhandle from under the bar. "Get
out of here, Cuban!"

So now Pablo knew the bartender didn't want him in the
bar. "Now, let me get this straight. If I ask you for drink, and
you give me drink, you would break that glass too?"

"That's right. But you better not order again."

Pablo sighed. He was sad. "Well, then we will pretend I
got drunk in this bar." And the next thing anybody knew
Pablo was behind the bar, breaking all the glasses he could
reach.

"And we will pretend that I look at myself in your mirror."
He picked up a bottle and cracked the big mirror they had.

By now there was a regular riot going on with all the men
in the bar trying to catch and hold him, and Pablo running
around, breaking chairs and tables. Finally just before they

214   caught and tied him up, he tipped over their piano. "We will pretend I play a Cuban song on this piano!"

They called the police and held him until the wagon came. And the next time I saw him was in court the next morning, where the judge kept looking at Pablo like he really didn't believe that a man who seemed so kind and gentle could do such things. But it was plain Pablo had wrecked the Irishman's bar. The judge sentenced him to thirty days in the city jail, and fifty dollars damages, which Pablo couldn't pay. So the judge gave him thirty extra days.

I didn't see Pablo for the next two months. When he came home, he was changed. He wasn't smiling at all, and you remember that he used to smile all the time. As soon as he came in the house he told me he was going out again. I knew where and I got mad. "Do you want to spend another two months in jail? Is that what you want?"

He didn't understand me. "Why you ask me that?"

"Why! You're going over there to that white man's bar and get into a fight and go on back to jail. Did you like it that much? Did jail change you so much?"

"Jennie, don't you see? I try not to change." He picked up five boxes of cigars he'd made before he went to jail and put them into a brown paper bag, and tucked the bag under his arm.

I watched him go out the door and then started to cry. I loved him, you see, and didn't want him back in jail. And I cried because I didn't understand him now and was afraid of that.

When the Irishmen saw him coming into their bar, they were stunned. Their mouths dropped open and they all got very quiet. Pablo didn't pay them any mind, just walked up to the bar and put his foot on the brass rail.

The bartender picked up his axhandle. "What you want 215
here, Cuban? Ain't you had enough?"

"No." Pablo didn't smile. He took the brown paper bag
and put it gently on the counter. Cigars, he said, are delicate
and shouldn't be tossed around.

The bartender looked at the bag. "What you got there?"

"Maybe you find out." He touched the box with his fingers.
"I like a drink."

The bartender stared at him for a second and then at the
paper bag for a long time. He started to sweat. "All right."
He set the drink down in front of Pablo.

For a minute, Pablo just looked at it. Then he lifted it to
his lips and drank it down and pushed it across the bar to
the bartender.

The bartender picked it up and studied it. Finally, he
looked at Pablo again. "What the hell! I had to close up for
a week after you was here the first time." He took the glass
to the sink, washed it with soap and water, and put it with
the other clean glasses. Then he looked at Pablo again.
"Satisfied?"

"Not yet." Pablo grabbed the paper bag and started to
open it.

"Watch out, fellows!" The bartender yelled in his ear.
When Pablo looked up, all the men in the bar were lying on
their stomachs covering their heads. The bartender was behind the bar on his knees, his hands over his ears.

Pablo took a cigar box out of the bag, opened it, pulled
himself up and across the bar, and reached the box down to
the bartender. "Hey, you want fine, handmade Havana
cigar?" He was smiling.

"Are you going back down to that corner?" My grandmother took my hand.

I looked into her face and then at the picture of her husband. He was still studying something just above my head. "I guess so." I did not really want to do it.

"You may not even have to use that." She pointed at the broom handle. "But you should know you can."

I knew this was true and climbed off the bed and picked up the white hat and the broom handle. "Okay."

"I'll be waiting on the porch for you." She smiled, got up, and, sighing, went out to the kitchen.

For a while, I listened to pots knocking and being filled with water. Then I stood in her room and practiced what I would say to Valentine's Gang: "If you guys don't let me go by, I'll have to hit you with this." There was a quake in my voice the first time I said it out loud, but, if I had to, I thought I would actually be able to say it and then use the stick. I went down the hall, onto the porch, and looked down toward the corner.

It was empty. The mothers of the members of Valentine's Gang had summoned them home to supper.

About the Author

William Melvin Kelley was born in New York City in 1937. He studied at Harvard University, where he began his first very successful novel, *A Different Drummer,* a semifantastic story about what happens to a southern state when the entire black population decides to move out. Subsequently, Kelley won several literary awards and fellowships. He has published four books and also stories in such magazines as *The Saturday Evening Post, Negro Digest, Esquire,* and *Mademoiselle.* He has taught at the State University of New York.

"Enemy Territory" is one of a group of stories largely based on his own boyhood experiences. Most of his published work deals with the situation of black people in America, particularly with their relationship to the white population.

FOR DISCUSSION

The events in this story move Tommy from a child's world and a child's character to a different world.

1. What do the following parts of the story tell you about Tommy before his grandmother helped him to change?

    a. The way Tommy was playing at the beginning.

    b. The kind of thoughts Tommy had as he approached the Valentine Gang.

    c. The words Tommy shouted at the gang after he returned to his own side of the street.

    d. The way he *expected* his grandmother to behave when he got back to the house.

2. Why did his grandmother behave as she did when Tommy got back?

3. What does his grandmother really mean when she says, "Speak softly and carry a big stick"?

4. Do you think the story about Pablo contradicts the idea that people ought to be peaceful and gentle? Support your answer by specific references to the character of Pablo and the events in the story. Consider the following:

    a. Pablo's character at home and among friends.

    b. His behavior in the Irish bar.

    c. His decision to return to the bar when he left jail.

    d. The box of cigars and what he did with it.

5. What kind of feelings do you suppose the Irish bartender had about Pablo *after* Pablo's second visit to the bar?

6. How would you sum up what Tommy should have learned from the story of Pablo? Include the importance of Pablo's box of cigars in your answer.

7. How was the Tommy at the end of the story different from the Tommy at the beginning?

VOCABULARY GROWTH

One of the marks of the superior storyteller is his use of sharp, clear, specific words.

Sentences from "Enemy Territory" appear below, first as the author wrote them (with one word in italics), and then with a different word substituted for the author's word.

Using a dictionary, explain the difference between each pair of words in italics. Which word is better?

1. a. "I *peered* over a rotting tree stump and saw him moving, without a helmet, in the bushes."
   b. I *looked* over a rotting tree stump and saw him moving, without a helmet, in the bushes.

2. a. "As I had waited in ambush for Jerome, I had seen Mr. Bixby . . . *chug* down the steps."
   b. As I had waited in ambush for Jerome, I had seen Mr. Bixby . . . *walk* down the steps.

3. a. "I *scooped up* the hat." b. I *picked up* the hat.

4. a. "But even as I *ranted* at them, I could see I was doing so in vain."
   b. But even as I *shouted* at them, I could see I was doing so in vain.

FOR COMPOSITION

1. Do you think Pablo acted intelligently or stupidly on his *first* visit to the bar. Explain your answer in a composition.

2. Write a composition in which you explain what the Irish bartender must have learned from Pablo.

The New Kid

MURRAY HEYERT

If you haven't been part of a scene like this,
you have observed it: the boys are choosing up
sides for a ball game and there's one boy
nobody seems to want. You can guess how he
feels. But this story has an unusual twist.

BY THE time Marty ran up the stairs, past the
dentist's office, where it smelled like the time his father was
in the hospital, past the fresh paint smell, where the new
kid lived, past the garlic smell from the Italians in 2D; and
waited for Mommer to open the door; and threw his school-
books on top of the old newspapers that were piled on the
sewing machine in the hall; and drank his glass of milk
("How many times must I tell you not to gulp! Are you
going to stop gulping like that or must I smack your face!");
and set the empty glass in the sink under the faucet; and
changed into his brown keds; and put trees into his school
shoes ("How many times must I talk to you! God in Heaven
—when will you learn to take care of your clothes and not
make me follow you around like this!"); and ran downstairs

219

again, past the garlic and the paint and the hospital smells; by the time he got into the street and looked breathlessly around him, it was too late. The fellows were all out there, all ready for a game, and just waiting for Eddie Deakes to finish chalking a base against the curb.

Running up the street with all his might, Marty could see that the game would start any minute now. Out in the gutter Paulie Dahler was tossing high ones to Ray-Ray Stickerling, whose father was a bus driver and sometimes gave the fellows transfers so they could ride free. The rest were sitting on the curb, waiting for Eddie to finish making the base and listening to Gelberg, who was a Jew, explain what it meant to be bar-mitzvah'd, like he was going to be next month.

They did not look up as Marty galloped up to them all out of breath. Eddie finished making his base and after looking at it critically a moment, with his head on one side, moved down toward the sewer that was home plate and began drawing a scoreboard alongside it. With his nose running from excitement Marty trotted over to him.

"Just going to play with two bases?" he said, wiping his nose on the sleeve of his lumber jacket, and hoping with all his might that Eddie would think he had been there all the while and was waiting for a game like all the other fellows.

Eddie raised his head and saw that it was Marty. He gave Marty a shove. "Why don't you watch where you're walking?" he said. "Can't you see I'm making a scoreboard!"

He bent over again and with his chalk repaired the lines that Marty had smudged with his sneakers. Marty hopped around alongside him, taking care to keep his feet off the chalked box. "Gimme a game, Eddie?" he said.

"What are you asking me for?" Eddie said, without looking up. "It ain't my game."

"Aw, come on, Eddie. I'll get even on you!" Marty said.

"Ask Gelberg. It's his game," Eddie said, straightening himself and shoving his chalk into his pants pocket. He trotted suddenly into the middle of the street and ran sideways a few feet. "Here go!" he hollered. "All the way!"

From his place up near the corner Paulie Dahler heaved the ball high into the air, higher than the telephone wires. Eddie took a step back, then a step forward, then back again, and got under it.

Marty bent his knees like a catcher, pounded his fist into his palm as though he were wearing a mitt, and held out his hands. "Here go, Eddie!" he hollered. "Here go!"

Holding the ball in his hand, and without answering him, Eddie walked toward the curb, where the rest of the fellows were gathered around Gelberg. Marty straightened his knees, put down his hands, and sniffing his nose, trotted after Eddie.

"All right, I'll choose Gelberg for sides," Eddie said.

Gelberg heaved himself off the curb and put on his punchball glove, which was one of his mother's old kid gloves, with the fingers and thumb cut off short. "Odds, once takes it," he said.

After a couple of preparatory swings of their arms they matched fingers. Gelberg won. He chose Albie Newbauer. Eddie looked around him and took Wally Reinhard. Gelberg took Ray-Ray Stickerling. Eddie took Wally Reinhard's brother, Howey.

Marty hopped around on the edge of the group. "Hey, Gelberg," he hollered, in a high voice. "Gimme a game, will you?"

"I got Arnie," Gelberg said.

Eddie looked around him again. "All right, I got Paulie Dahler."

They counted their men. "Choose you for up first," Gelberg said. Feeling as though he were going to cry, Marty watched them as they swung their arms, stuck out their fingers. This time Eddie won. Gelberg gathered his men around him and they trotted into the street to take up positions on the field. They hollered "Here go!" threw the ball from first to second, then out into the field, and back again to Gelberg in the pitcher's box.

Marty ran over to him. "Gimme a game, will you, Gelberg?"

"We're all choosed up," Gelberg said, heaving a high one to Arnie out in center field.

Marty wiped his nose on his sleeve. "Come on, gimme a game. Didn't I let you lose my Spaulding Hi-Bouncer down the sewer once?"

"Want to give the kid a game?" Gelberg called to Eddie, who was seated on the curb, figuring out his batting order with his men.

"Aw, we got the sides all choosed up!" Eddie said.

Marty stuck out his lower lip and wished that he would not have to cry. "You give Howey Reinhard a game!" he said, pointing at Howey sitting on the curb next to Eddie. "He can't play any better than me!"

"Yeah," Howey yelled, swinging back his arm as though he were going to punch Marty in the jaw. "You couldn't hit the side of the house!"

"Yeah, I can play better than you any day!" Marty hollered.

"You can play left outside!" Howey said, looking around to see how the joke went over.

"Yeah, I'll get even on you!" Marty hollered, hoping that maybe they would get worried and give him a game after all.

With a fierce expression on his face, as if to indicate that he was through joking and now meant serious business, Howey sprang up from the curb and sent him staggering with a shove. Marty tried to duck, but Howey smacked him across the side of the head. Flinging his arms up about his ears Marty scrambled down the street; for no reason at all Paulie Dahler booted him in the pants as he went by.

"I'll get even on you!" Marty yelled, when he was out of reach. With a sudden movement of his legs Howey pretended to rush at him. Almost falling over himself in panic Marty dashed toward the house, but stopped, feeling ashamed, when he saw that Howey had only wanted to make him run.

For a while he stood there on the curb, wary and ready to dive into the house the instant any of the fellows made a move toward him. But presently he saw that the game was beginning, and that none of them was paying any more attention to him. He crept toward them again, and seating himself on the curb a little distance away, watched the game start. For a moment he thought of breaking it up, rushing up to the scoreboard and smudging it with his sneakers before anyone could stop him, and then dashing into the house before they caught him. Or grabbing the ball when it came near him and flinging it down the sewer. But he decided not to; the fellows would catch him in the end, smack him and make another scoreboard or get another ball, and then he would never get a game.

Every minute feeling more and more like crying, he sat there on the curb, his elbow on his knee, his chin in his palm, and tried to think where he could get another fellow, so that they could give him a game and still have even

224   sides. Then he lifted his chin from his palm and saw that the new kid was sitting out on the stoop in front of the house, chewing something and gazing toward the game; and all at once the feeling that he was going to cry disappeared. He sprang up from the curb.

"Hey, Gelberg!" he hollered. "If I get the new kid for even sides can I get a game?"

Without waiting for an answer he dashed down the street toward the stoop where the new kid was sitting.

"Hey, fellow!" he shouted. "Want a game? Want a game of punchball?"

He could see now that what the new kid was eating was a slice of rye bread covered with apple sauce. He could see, too, that the new kid was smaller than he was, and had a narrow face and a large nose with a few little freckles across the bridge. He was wearing Boy Scout pants and a brown woolen pullover, and on the back of his head was a skullcap made from the crown of a man's felt hat, the edge turned up and cut into sharp points that were ornamented with brass paper clips.

All out of breath he stopped in front of the new kid. "What do you say?" he hollered. "Want a game?"

The new kid looked at him and took another bite of rye bread. "I don't know," he said, with his mouth full of bread, turning to take another look at the fellows in the street. "I guess I got to go to the store soon."

"You don't have to go to the store right away, do you?" Marty said, in a high voice.

The new kid swallowed his bread and continued looking up toward the game. "I got to stay in front of the house in case my mother calls me."

"Maybe she won't call you for a while," Marty said. He could see that the inning was ending, that they would be starting a new inning in a minute, and his legs twitched with impatience.

"I don't know," the new kid said, still looking up at the game. "Anyway, I got my good shoes on."

"Aw, I bet you can't even play punchball!" cried Marty.

The new kid looked at him with his lower lip stuck out. "Yeah, I can so play! Only I got to go to the store!"

Once more he looked undecidedly up toward the game. Marty could see that the inning was over now. He turned pleadingly to the new kid.

"You can hear her if she calls you, can't you? Can't you play just till she calls you? Come on, can't you?"

Putting the last of his rye bread into his mouth, the new kid got up from the stoop. "Well, when she calls me—" he said, brushing off the seat of his pants with his hand, "when she calls me I got to quit and go to the store."

As fast as he could run Marty dashed up the street with the new kid trailing after him. "Hey, I got another man for even sides!" he yelled. "Gimme a game now? I got another man!"

The fellows looked at the new kid coming up the street behind Marty.

"You new on the block?" Howey Reinhard asked, eyeing the Boy Scout pants, as Marty and the new kid came up to them.

"You any good?" Gelberg demanded, bouncing the ball at his feet and looking at the skullcap ornamented with brass paper clips. "Can you hit?"

"Come on!" Marty said. He wished that they would just give him a game and not start asking a lot of questions. "I got another man for even sides, didn't I?"

"Aw, we got the game started already!" Ray-Ray Sticker-ling hollered.

Marty sniffled his nose, which was beginning to run again, and looked at him as fiercely as he was able. "It ain't your game!" he yelled. "It's Gelberg's game! Ain't it your game, Gelberg?"

Gelberg gave him a shove. "No one said you weren't going to get a game!" With a last bounce of his ball he turned to Eddie, who was looking the new kid over carefully.

"All right, Eddie. I'll take the new kid and you can have Marty."

Eddie drew his arm back as though he were going to hit him. "Like fun! Why don't you take Marty, if you're so wise?"

"I won the choose-up!" Gelberg hollered.

"Yeah, that was before! I'm not taking Marty!"

"I won the choose-up, didn't I?"

"Well, you got to choose up again for the new kid!"

Marty watched them as they stood up to each other, each eying the other suspiciously, and swung their arms to choose. Eddie won. "Cheating shows!" he yelled, seizing the new kid by the arm, and pulling him into the group on his side.

Trying to look like the ball players he had seen the time his father had taken him to the Polo Grounds, Marty ran into the outfield and took the position near the curb that Gelberg had selected for him. He tried not to feel bad because Eddie had taken the new kid, that no one knew anything about, how he could hit, or anything; and that he had had to go to the loser of the choose-up. As soon as he was out in the field he leaned forward, with his hands propped on his knees, and hollered: "All right, all right, these guys can't hit!" Then he straightened up and pounded his fist into his palm as though he were wearing a fielder's glove and shouted: "Serve it to them on a silver platter, Gelberg! These guys are just a bunch of fan artists!" He propped his hands on his knees again, like a big-leaguer, but all the while he felt unhappy, not nearly the way he should have felt, now that they had finally given him a game. He hoped that they would hit to him, and he would make one-handed catches over his head, run way out with his back to the ball and spear them blind, or run in with all his might and pick them right off the tops of his shoes.

A little nervous chill ran through his back as he saw Paulie Dahler get up to hit. On Gelberg's second toss Paulie stepped in and sent the ball sailing into the air. A panic seized Marty as he saw it coming at him. He took a step nervously forward, then backward, then forward again, trying as hard as he could to judge the ball. It smacked into his cupped palms, bounced out and dribbled toward the curb. He scrambled after it, hearing them shouting at him, and feeling himself getting more scared every instant. He kicked the ball with his sneaker, got his hand on it, and straightening himself in a fever of fright, heaved it with all his strength at Ray-Ray on first. The moment the ball left his hand he knew he had done the wrong thing. Paulie was already on his way to second; and besides, the throw was wild. Ray-Ray leaped into the air, his arms flung up, but it was way over his head, bouncing beyond him on the sidewalk and almost hitting a woman who was jouncing a baby carriage at the door of the apartment house opposite.

With his heart beating the same way it did whenever anyone chased him, Marty watched Paulie gallop across the plate. He sniffled his nose, which was beginning to run again, and felt like crying.

"Holy Moses!" he heard Gelberg yell. "What do you want, a basket? Can't you hold on to them once in a while?"

"Aw, the sun was in my eyes!" Marty said.

"You wait until you want another game!" Gelberg shouted.

Breathing hard, Ray-Ray got back on first and tossed the ball to Gelberg. "Whose side are you on anyway?" he hollered.

Eddie Deakes put his hands to his mouth like a megaphone. "Attaboy, Marty!" he yelled. "Having you out there is like having another man on our side!"

The other fellows on the curb laughed, and Howey Reinhard made them laugh harder by pretending to catch a fly ball with the sun in his eyes, staggering around the street with his eyes screwed up and his hands cupped like a sissy, so that the wrists touched and the palms were widely separated.

No longer shouting or punching his fist into his palm, Marty took his place out in the field again. He stood there, feeling like crying, and wished that he hadn't dropped that ball, or thrown it over Ray-Ray's head. Then, without knowing why, he looked up to see whether the new kid was laughing at him like all the rest. But the new kid was sitting a little off by himself at one end of the row of fellows on the curb, and with a serious expression on his face gnawed at the skin at the side of his thumbnail. Marty began to wonder if the new kid was any good or not. He saw him sitting there, with the serious look on his face, his ears sticking out, not joking like the other fellows, and from nowhere the thought leaped into Marty's head that maybe the new kid was no good. He looked at the skinny legs, the Boy Scout pants, and the mama's boy shoes and all at once he began to hope that Eddie would send the new kid in to hit, so that he could know right away whether he was any good or not.

But Wally Reinhard was up next. He fouled out on one of Gelberg's twirls, and after him Howey popped up to Albie Newbauer and Eddie was out on first. The fellows ran in to watch Eddie chalk up Paulie's run on the scoreboard alongside the sewer. They were still beefing and hollering at Marty for dropping that ball, but he pretended he did not hear them and sat down on the curb to watch the new kid out in the field.

He was over near the curb, playing in closer than Paulie Dahler. Marty could see that he was not hollering "Here go!" or "All the way!" like the others, but merely stood there with that serious expression on his face and watched them throw the ball around. He held one leg bent at the ankle, so that the side of his shoe rested on the pavement, his belly was stuck out, and he chewed the skin at the side of his thumbnail.

Gelberg got up to bat. Standing in the pitcher's box, Eddie turned around and motioned his men to lay out. The new kid looked around him to see what the other fellows did, took a few steps backward, and then, with his belly stuck out again, went on chewing his thumb.

Marty felt his heart begin to beat hard. He watched Gelberg stand up to the plate and contemptuously fling back the first few pitches.

"Come on, gimme one like I like!" Gelberg hollered.

"What's the matter! You afraid to reach for them?" Eddie yelled.

"Just pitch them to me, that's all!" Gelberg said.

Eddie lobbed one in that bounced shoulder high. With a little sideways skip Gelberg lammed into it.

The ball sailed down toward the new kid. Feeling his heart begin to beat harder, Marty saw him take a hurried

230 step backward, and at the same moment fling his hands before his face and duck his head. The ball landed beyond him and bounded up on the sidewalk. For an instant the new kid hesitated, then he was galloping after it, clattering across the pavement in his polished shoes.

Swinging his arms in mock haste, Gelberg breezed across the plate. "Get a basket!" he hollered over his shoulder. "Get a basket!"

Marty let his nose run without bothering to sniffle. He jumped up from the curb and curved his hands around his mouth like a megaphone. "He's scared of the ball!" he yelled at the top of his lungs. "He's scared of the ball! That's what he is, scared of the ball!"

The new kid tossed the ball back to Eddie. "I wasn't scared!" he said, moistening his lips with his tongue. "I wasn't scared! I just couldn't see it coming!"

With an expression of despair on his face Eddie shook his head. "Holy Moses! If you can't see the ball why do you try to play punchball?" He bounced the ball hard at his feet and motioned Gelberg to send in his next batter. Arnie got up from the curb and wiping his hands on his pants walked toward the plate.

Marty felt his heart pounding in his chest. He hopped up and down with excitement and seizing Gelberg by the arm pointed at the new kid.

"You see him duck?" he yelled. "He's scared of the ball, that's what he is!" He hardly knew where to turn first. He rushed up to Ray-Ray, who was sitting on the curb making marks on the asphalt with the heel of his sneaker. "The new kid's scared to stop a ball! You see him duck!"

The new kid looked toward Marty and wet his lips with his tongue. "Yeah," he yelled, "didn't you muff one that was right in your hands?"

He was looking at Marty with a sore expression on his face, and his lower lip stuck out; and a sinking feeling went through Marty, a sudden sick feeling that maybe he had started something he would be sorry for. Behind him on the curb he could hear the fellows sniggering in that way they did when they picked on him. In the pitcher's box Eddie let out a loud cackling laugh.

"Yeah, the new kid's got your number!"

"The sun was in my eyes!" Marty said. He could feel his face getting red, and in the field the fellows were laughing. A wave of self-pity flowed through him.

"What are you picking on me for!" he yelled, in a high voice. "The sun was so in my eyes. Anyway, I ain't no yellow-belly! I wasn't scared of the ball!"

The instant he said it he was sorry. He sniffled his nose uneasily as he saw Gelberg look at Ray-Ray. For an instant he thought of running into the house before anything happened. But instead he just stood there, sniffling his nose and feeling his heart beating, fast and heavy.

"You hear what he called you?" Paulie Dahler yelled at the new kid.

"You're not going to let him get away with calling you a yellowbelly, are you?" Eddie said, looking at the new kid.

The new kid wet his lips with his tongue and looked at Marty. "I wasn't scared!" he said. He shifted the soles of his new-looking shoes on the pavement. "I wasn't scared! I just couldn't see it coming, that's all!"

Eddie was walking toward the new kid now, bouncing the ball slowly in front of him as he walked. In a sudden panic Marty looked back toward the house where old lady Kipnis lived. She always broke up fights; maybe she would break up this one; maybe she wouldn't even let it get started. But she wasn't out on her porch. He sniffled his nose, and

232 with all his might hoped that the kid's mother would call him to go to the store.

"Any kid that lets himself be called a yellowbelly must be a yellowbelly!" Albie Newbauer said, looking around him for approval.

"Yeah," Gelberg said. "I wouldn't let anyone call me a yellowbelly."

With a sudden shove Eddie sent the new kid scrambling forward toward Marty. He tried to check himself by stiffening his body and twisting to one side, but it was no use. Before he could recover his balance another shove made him stagger forward.

Marty sniffled his nose and looked at the kid's face close in front of him. It seemed as big as the faces he saw in the movies; and he could see that the kid's nose was beginning to run just like his own; and he could see in the corner of his mouth a crumb of the rye bread he had eaten on the stoop. For a moment the kid's eyes looked squarely into Marty's, so that he could see the little dark specks in the colored part around the pupil. Then the glance slipped away to one side; and all at once Marty had a feeling that the new kid was afraid of him.

"You gonna let him get away with calling you a yellow-belly?" he heard Eddie say. From the way it sounded he knew that the fellows were on his side now. He stuck out his jaw and waited for the new kid to answer.

"I got to go to the store!" the new kid said. There was a scared look on his face and he took a step back from Marty.

Paulie Dahler got behind him and shoved him against Marty. Although he tried not to, Marty couldn't help flinging his arms up before his face. But the new kid only backed away and kept his arms at his sides. A fierce excitement went through Marty as he saw how scared the look on the kid's face was. He thrust his chest up against the new kid.

"Yellowbelly!" he hollered, making his voice sound tough. "Scared of the ball!"

The new kid backed nervously away, and there was a look on his face as though he wanted to cry.

"Yeah, he's scared!" Eddie yelled.

"Slam him, Marty!" Wally Reinhard hollered. "The kid's scared of you!"

"Aw, sock the yellowbelly!" Marty heard Gelberg say, and he smacked the kid as hard as he could on the shoulder. The kid screwed up his face to keep from crying, and tried to back through the fellows ringed around him.

"Lemme alone!" he yelled.

Marty looked at him fiercely, with his jaw thrust forward, and felt his heart beating. He smacked the kid again, making him stagger against Arnie in back of him.

"Yeah, yellowbelly!" Marty hollered, feeling how the fellows were on his side, and how scared the new kid was. He began smacking him again and again on the shoulder.

"Three, six, nine, a bottle of wine, I can fight you any old time!" he yelled. With each word he smacked the kid on the shoulder or arm. At the last word he swung with all his strength. He meant to hit the kid on the shoulder, but at the last instant, even while his arm was swinging, something compelled him to change his aim; his fist caught the kid on the mouth with a hard, wet, socking sound. The shock of his knuckles against the kid's mouth, and that sound of it, made Marty want to hit him again and again. He put his head down and began swinging wildly, hitting the new kid without any aim on the head and shoulders and arms.

The new kid buried his head in his arms and began to cry. "Lemme alone!" he yelled. He tried to rush through the fellows crowded around him.

With all his might Marty smacked him on the side of the head. Rushing up behind him Arnie smacked him too. Paulie Dahler shoved the skullcap, with its paper clip ornaments, over the kid's eyes; and as he went by Gelberg booted him in the pants.

Crying and clutching his cap the new kid scampered over to the curb out of reach.

"I'll get even on you!" he cried.

With a fierce expression on his face Marty made a sudden movement of his legs and pretended to rush at him. The kid threw his arms about his head and darted down the street toward the house. When he saw that Marty was not coming after him he sat down on the stoop; and Marty could see him rubbing his knuckles against his mouth.

Howey Reinhard was making fun of the new kid, scampering up and down the pavement with his arms wrapped around his head and hollering, "Lemme alone! Lemme alone!" The fellows laughed, and although he was breathing hard, and his hand hurt from hitting the kid, Marty had to laugh too.

"You see him duck when that ball came at him?" he panted at Paulie Dahler.

Paulie shook his head. "Boy, just wait until we get the yellowbelly in the schoolyard!"

"And on Halloween," Gelberg said. "Wait until we get him on Halloween with our flour stockings!" He gave Marty a little shove and made as though he were whirling an imaginary flour stocking round his head.

Standing there in the middle of the street, Marty suddenly thought of Halloween, of the winter and snowballs,

of the schoolyard. He saw himself whirling a flour stocking **235**
around his head and rushing at the new kid, who scampered
in terror before him hollering, "Lemme alone! Lemme alone!"
As clearly as if it were in the movies, he saw himself flinging
snowballs and the new kid backed into a corner of the
schoolyard, with his hands over his face. Before he knew
what he was doing, Marty turned fiercely toward the stoop
where the new kid was still sitting, rubbing his mouth and
crying.

"Hey, yellowbelly!" Marty hollered; and he pretended
he was going to rush at the kid.

Almost falling over himself in fright the new kid scrambled inside the house. Marty stood in the middle of the street
and sniffled his nose. He shook his fist at the empty doorway.

"You see him run?" he yelled, so loud that it made his
throat hurt. "Boy, you see him run?" He stood there shaking
his fist, although the new kid was no longer there to see him.
He could hardly wait for the winter, for Halloween, or the
very next day in the schoolyard.

About the Author

Murray Heyert's story is based on his own early years in the
Bronx streets of New York, where he was born in 1912. He attended public schools and New York University, later working
as a civilian technician with the Air Force and for private
industry. He has published several essays and stories.

FOR DISCUSSION

Understanding the Characters

1. Put yourself in Marty's place when he can't get into the game. How would you have felt? What do you suppose Marty's life on this street must have been like in the past?

2. Why is Marty so active all the time—jumping, moving about, talking, shouting? If you can answer this question correctly, you are an expert psychologist.

3. What thoughts about the "new kid" occurred to you when he said he had to go to the store, he had to wait for his mother, he had new shoes?

4. How do you explain Marty's especially bad handling of the fly ball that came to him?

5. When the new boy missed the ball, how did Marty react, in comparison with the other boys? Did his behavior then seem real and natural to you? Explain your answer.

6. Were you shocked at Marty's behavior at the close of the story, or did you expect it? Explain why you reacted as you did.

Understanding the Theme

No one in this story states a theme. The author lets the facts speak for themselves. But a good reader will realize that the author had something to say about human behavior and human character. See if you can arrive at the theme by answering these questions.

1. At the start of the story, what did Marty need that he clearly was not getting?

2. Whom would you blame for Marty's situation? Why?

3. In some ways the "new kid" might have been a natural friend for Marty. Why?

4. Why then did Marty treat him as he did? (The answer is not a simple one. Consider Marty's past, his needs, the effect of the behavior of the other boys.)

5. Do boys in real life treat each other as Marty and the new kid were treated, or does this story give a false picture?

Do girls behave the same way or differently?

6. Can you think of any ways in which such treatment can be prevented or stopped? Or will children always behave this way? Explain your answer.

7. Keeping in mind the answers given to the preceding questions, try to state the theme of the story in a few carefully worded sentences.

Understanding the Author's Art

1. Nowhere does the writer *tell* us about the characters of Marty, or the "new kid," or the other boys. And yet we have a good idea of the kind of person each one was. To appreciate how the author let us know without *telling* us, list the character traits of Marty, and then indicate how you realized each trait as the story went along.

2. Would you have preferred that the author *tell* you the character of Marty—that he write, for example, "Marty was unhappy because the boys did not let him play with them," or "Marty was anxious to be recognized as one of the boys. He felt very inferior because he had not been accepted"? Or did you like Mr. Heyert's method of characterization, which required you to draw your own conclusions? Explain your answer.

VOCABULARY GROWTH

Appreciating the Author's Choice of Words

Each italicized word in the following sentences from the story tells something important about the person or people being described. Look up the word in the dictionary, and explain why that word particularly suits the person or the people referred to, *at that moment in the story.*

1. "For a while, he [Marty] stood there on the curb, *wary* and ready to dive into the house the instant any of the fellows made a move toward him." (page 223)

2. "As soon as he was out in the field he [Marty] leaned forward, with his hands *propped* on his knees. . . ." (page 226)

3. "He watched Gelberg stand up to the plate and *contemptuously* fling back the first few pitches." (page 229)

4. "Behind him on the curb he could hear the fellows *sniggering* in that way they did when they picked on him." (page 231)

5. "Crying and clutching his cap the new kid *scampered* over to the curb out of reach." (page 234)

FOR COMPOSITION

1. Do you recall any incident in which a young person was cruelly treated by other young people? Describe the occasion, and tell how you feel about it now.

2. Many people say it is wrong to describe children as being cruel to one another. Are children perhaps more kind-hearted than this story seems to indicate? Write a composition in which you discuss this question, supporting your opinion by reference to your own experiences and friends.

3. Is this story only about children? Or are there evidences of the same characteristics among adults? Write a composition discussing this question, giving logical reasons to support your opinion.

Adjö Means Goodbye

CARRIE ALLEN YOUNG

Two wonderfully close friends . . . a birthday
party . . . the friendship broken forever. Yet there
was no quarrel, no reason you could see on the
surface.
What really happened?

IT HAS been a long time since I knew Marget Swenson. How the years have rushed by! I was a child when I knew
her, and now I myself have children. The circle keeps turning,
keeps coming full.

The mind loses many things as it matures, but I never lost
Marget; she has remained with me like the first love and the
first hurt. The mind does not lose what is meaningful to one's
existence. Marget was both my first love and first hurt. I met
her when she joined our sixth-grade class.

239

She stood before the class holding tightly to the teacher's hand, her blue, frightened eyes sweeping back and forth across the room until they came to rest on my face. From that very first day, we became friends. Marget, just fresh from Sweden, and I, a sixth generation American. We were both rather shy and quiet and perhaps even lonely, and that's why we took to each other. She spoke very little English, but somehow we managed to understand each other. We visited one another at home practically every day. My young life had suddenly become deliciously complete. I had a dear friend.

Sometimes we talked and laughed on the top of the big, dazzling green hill close to the school. We had so much to talk about; so many things were new to her. She asked a thousand questions and I—I, filled to bursting with pride that it was from me that she wished to learn, responded eagerly and with excesses of superlatives.

Now, sometimes, when I drive my children to school and watch them race up the walks to the doors, I wonder what lies ahead in the momentary darkness of the hall corridors and think of Marget once more. I think of how she came out of a dark corridor one day, the day she really looked at my brother when she was visiting me. I saw her following him with new eyes, puzzled eyes, and a strange fear gripped me. "Your brother," she whispered to me, "is African?"

I was a little surprised and a little hurt. Didn't we cheer for Tarzan when we went to the movies? Were not the Africans always frightened and cowardly? But I answered, "No, silly," and I continued to wait.

"He looks different from you."

"He should," I said, managing to laugh. My brother *was* darker than anyone else in the family. "He's a boy and I'm a girl. But we're both Negro, of course."

She opened her mouth to say something else, then closed it and the fear slipped away.

Marget lived up on the hill. That was the place where there were many large and pretty houses. I suppose it was only in passing that I knew only white people lived there. Whenever I visited, Marget's mother put up a table in their garden, and Marget and I had milk and *kaka*, a kind of cake. Mrs. Swenson loved to see me eat. She was a large, round woman with deep blue eyes and very red cheeks. Marget, though much smaller, of course, looked quite like her. We did our homework after we had the cake and milk, compositions or story reading. When we finished, Mrs. Swenson hugged me close and I knew I was loved in that home. A child knows when it is loved or only tolerated. But I was loved. Mrs. Swenson thanked me with a thick, Swedish accent for helping Marget.

Marget and I had so much fun with words, and there were times when we sat for hours in my garden or hers or on the hilltop, surrounded by grass and perhaps the smell of the suppers being prepared for our fathers still at work downtown. Her words were Swedish; mine, English. We were surprised how much alike many of them sounded, and we laughed at the way each of us slid our tongues over the unfamiliar words. I learned the Swedish equivalents of *mother, father, house, hello, friend,* and *goodbye.*

One day Marget and I raced out of school as soon as the ringing bell released us. We sped down the hill, flashed over gray concrete walks and green lawns dotted with dandelions and scattered daisies, our patent leather buckled shoes slapping a merry tattoo as we went, our long stockings tumbling down our legs. We were going to Marget's to plan her birthday party. Such important business for ten-year-olds!

Eventually, after much planning and waiting, the day of the party came. I put on my pink organdy dress with the Big Bertha collar and a new pair of patent leather shoes that tortured my feet unbearably. Skipping up the hill to Marget's, I stopped at a lawn which looked deserted. I set down my gift and began to pick the wild flowers that were growing there. Suddenly, from out of nowhere, an old man appeared. "What do you think you're doing pulling up my flowers?" he shouted. Once again I held myself tightly against the fear, awaiting that awful thing that I felt must come. "I wanted to take them to my friend," I explained. "She's having a birthday today."

The old man's eyes began to twinkle. "She is, is she? Well, you just wait a minute, young lady." He went away and came back with garden shears and cut a handful and then an armful of flowers, and with a smile sent me on my way. My childish fears had been ambushed by a kindness.

I arrived at the party early and Marget and I whizzed around, putting the finishing touches on the decorations. There were hardly enough vases for all the flowers the old man had given me. Some fifteen minutes later the doorbell rang, and Marget ran around to the front saying, "Oh, here they come!"

But it was Mary Ann, another girl in our class, and she was alone. She put her present for Marget on the table, and the three of us talked. Occasionally, Marget got up and went around to the front to see who had come unheralded by the doorbell. No one.

"I wonder what's taking them so long?" Mary Ann asked.

Growing more upset by the minute, Marget answered, "Maybe they didn't remember what time the party was."

How does a child of ten describe a sense of foreboding, **243** the feeling that the bad things have happened because of herself? I sat silently, waiting.

When it got to be after five, Mrs. Swenson called Marget inside; she was there for a long time, and when she came out, she looked very, very sad. "My mother does not think they are coming," she said.

"Why not?" Mary Ann blurted.

"Betty Hatcher's mother was here last night, and she talked a long time with my mother. I thought it was about the party. Mother kept saying, 'Yes, yes, she is coming'."

I took Marget's hand. "Maybe they were talking about me," I said. Oh! I remember so painfully today how I wanted her quick and positive denial to that thrust of mine into darkness where I knew something alive was lurking. Although she did it quite casually, I was aware that Marget was trying to slip her hand from mine, as though she might have had the same thought I had voiced aloud. I opened my hand and let her go. "Don't be silly," she said.

No one came. The three of us sat in the middle of rows and rows of flowers and ate our ice cream and cake. Our pretty dresses, ribbons and shoes were dejected blobs of color. It was as if the world had swung out around us and gone past, leaving us whole, but in some way indelibly stamped forever.

It was different between Marget and me after her birthday. She stopped coming to my house, and when at school I asked her when she would, she looked as though she would cry. She had to do something for her mother was her unvarying excuse. So, one day, I went to her house, climbed up the hill where the old man had picked the flowers, and

244 a brooding, restless thing grew within me at every step, almost a *knowing*. I had not, after all, been invited to Marget's. My throat grew dry and I thought about turning back, and for the first time the hill and all the homes looked alien, even threatening to me.

Marget almost jumped when she opened the door. She stared at me in shock. Then, quickly, in a voice I'd never heard before, she said, "My mother says you can't come to my house any more."

I opened my mouth, and closed it without speaking. The awful thing had come; the knowing was confirmed. Marget, crying, closed the door in my face. When I turned to go down the stairs and back down the hill to my house, my eyes, too, were filled with tears. No one had to tell me that the awful thing had come because Marget was white and I was not. I just *knew it* deep within myself. I guess I expected it to happen. It was only a question of when.

June. School was coming to a close. Those days brimmed with strange, uncomfortable moments when Marget and I looked at each other and our eyes darted quickly away. We were little pawns, one white, one colored, in a game over which we had no control then. We did not speak to each other at all.

On the last day of school, I screwed up a strange and reckless courage and took my autograph book to where Marget was sitting. I handed it to her. She hesitated, then took it, and without looking up, wrote words I don't remember now; they were quite common words, the kind every one was writing in every one else's book. I waited. Slowly, she passed her book to me and in it I wrote with a slow, firm hand some of the words she had taught me. I wrote *Adjö min vän*. Goodbye, my friend. I released her, let her go, told

her not to worry, told her that I no longer needed her. *Adjö.* **245**
Whenever I think of Marget now, and I do at the most surprising times, I wonder if she ever thinks of me, if she is married and has children, and I wonder if she has become a queen by now, instead of a pawn.

About the Author

Carrie Allen Young was born in Lynchburg, Virginia, but it was in Montclair, New Jersey, that she first saw a burning cross, the symbol of the Ku Klux Klan, the dreaded militant anti-black organization. She attended colleges in the South and the North. "Adjö Means Goodbye" is her first published story.

FOR DISCUSSION

Reading Below the Surface

You will recall that in many mature, artistic stories, the writer chooses to hint, to suggest, rather than to tell and explain everything. The good reader gets added pleasure from such stories because he can use his own intelligence and imagination to fill in the details the author is hinting at.

"Adjö Means Goodbye" is such a story. Below you will find some of the key sentences from the story which suggest information that is not directly expressed by the author. Each sentence is accompanied by a question that will test your ability to read beneath the surface.

Sometimes your knowledge of what happened later will

help you to grasp the real significance of a sentence that appears earlier in the story.

1. (Page 240) "We were both rather shy and quiet and perhaps even lonely, and that's why we took to each other."

   Why do you suppose the narrator of the story was lonely in her childhood days?

2. (Page 240) "Now sometimes, when I drive my children to school and watch them race up the walks to the doors, I wonder what lies ahead in the momentary darkness of the hall corridors."

   What is the narrator really wondering about in connection with her own children?

3. (Page 240) "I saw her following him with new eyes, puzzled eyes, and a strange fear gripped me. 'Your brother,' she whispered to me, 'is African'?"

   What do you learn from this about the color of the girl telling the story? Why was Marget her only friend?

4. (Page 241) "Marget lived up on the hill. That was the place where there were many large and pretty houses. I suppose it was only in passing that I knew only white people lived there."

   What conclusions can you draw about the narrator's house and the neighborhood she lived in?

5. (Page 243) "My mother does not think they are coming," she [Marget] said.

   "Why not?" Mary Ann blurted.

   "Betty Hatcher's mother was here last night, and she talked a long time with my mother. . . . Mother kept saying, 'Yes, yes, she is coming'."

   What did Betty Hatcher's mother talk about with Marget's mother?

   Who was the *she* in Mrs. Swenson's remark, "Yes, yes, she is coming."? What was the result of Mrs. Hatcher's visit?

6. (Page 243) "Although she did it quite casually, I was

aware that Marget was trying to slip her hand from mine."

What was the real importance of Marget's "slipping her hand from mine"?

7. (Page 244) "The awful thing had come; the knowing was confirmed. Marget, crying, had closed the door in my face."

Who was responsible for breaking the friendship? What were Marget's feelings about the situation?

8. (Page 244) "We were little pawns, one white, one colored, in a game over which we had no control." (In the game of chess, the pawns are the less important pieces that are moved around freely. The important pieces are the king and queen.)

What is the narrator suggesting about the real reason that the girls' friendship was broken up? Whom, if anyone, is she blaming? Explain your answer.

9. (Page 244) "I wrote Adjö min vän. Goodbye, my friend. I released her, let her go, told her not to worry, told her that I no longer needed her. Adjö."

What change had taken place in the narrator when she wrote this note? What was she saying about herself and her feeling about being a Negro girl?

10. "I wonder if she [Marget] has become a queen by now, instead of a pawn."

What is the difference in real life between being a king or queen and being just a pawn?

Understanding the Theme

1. What light does this story cast on this question: Are children born with race prejudices or do they learn to be prejudiced?

2. The narrator speaks several times of a fear that kept returning to her as she met different people. What fears do children in her situation have in a town like hers?

3. When the girl wrote "Adjö min vän" in Marget's auto-

graph book, was she better or worse off than she was at the opening of the story? Explain your answer.

4. At the conclusion of the story, the narrator speaks of adults as queens or pawns.

   a. In what ways are many white adults just pawns in their relations with and thoughts about black people?
   b. How can these people make themselves kings or queens in their relations with black people?
   c. In what ways can black people be pawns when they are adults?
   d. In what ways can black people make themselves kings or queens?

VOCABULARY GROWTH

Words in our language often have several meanings, some similar, some completely different. An important skill in using the dictionary is to select from all the definitions offered the one that fits and makes sense in the sentence where you found the word you are looking up.

Below are a number of sentences from the story, in each of which one word is italicized. For each such italicized word, several dictionary meanings are provided. In each case choose the meaning that best fits in the sentence from the story.

1. "A child knows when it is loved or only *tolerated*."
   tolerate: **a.** not interfere with
   b. respect without necessarily agreeing   **c.** put up with

2. "I learned the Swedish *equivalents* of mother, father, house, hello, friend, and goodbye."
   equivalent: **a.** equal in quantity   **b.** equal in force
   c. equal in meaning

3. "Although she did it quite *casually*, I was aware that Marget was trying to slip her hand from mine."
   casual: **a.** unplanned   **b.** occasional   **c.** careless

4. ". . . for the first time the hill and all the homes looked *alien*, even threatening to me."

alien: **a.** an outsider   **b.** owing allegiance to a foreign   **249**
country   **c.** strange

5. "The awful thing had come; the knowing was *confirmed.*
Marget, crying, closed the door in my face."
confirm: **a.** strengthen   **b.** prove the truth of
c. admit to full membership in the church

6. "We were little *pawns,* one white, one colored, in a
game over which we had no control then."
pawn: **a.** a chessman of the lowest value   **b.** (symbol) a
tool or a person subject to the will of another   **c.** anything given as security for a debt

FOR COMPOSITION

1. Have you ever first felt affection or love and then felt
hurt in your relations with someone. Tell what happened
in a composition.

2. Think about your experiences with young persons you
have met of another race or religion. Have these experiences made you feel friendly or antagonistic? Tell about
the experiences and your feelings in a composition.

3. Do you think it would be good or bad if young people
of different races and religions were able to meet and
mix freely without interference from adults? Write a
composition answering this question.

STORIES
OF
THE
FUTURE

The Rocket Man

RAY BRADBURY

Mercury . . . Venus . . . Mars . . . Jupiter. These are some of the planets Man may one day be visiting, traveling almost 500 *million* miles from his "home base" on Earth.

What makes men want to venture so far into space, with all the attendant dangers and hardships? And have you ever imagined what it must have been like for the wives, mothers, and children of the first astronauts who ventured, for example, to the moon, knowing that their loved ones might never return; that they might be lost forever, orbiting somewhere in space or stranded on the dead surface of the moon?

These are some of the questions raised in this story by Ray Bradbury, one of our foremost writers of science fiction. As clues in the story indicate, it takes place some time in the earlier part of the twenty-first century—perhaps about fifty years from now.

THE ELECTRICAL fireflies were hovering above Mother's dark hair to light her path. She stood in her bedroom door looking out at me as I passed in the silent hall. "You *will* help me keep him here this time, won't you?" she asked.

"I guess so," I said.

"Please." The fireflies cast moving bits of light on her white face. "This time he mustn't go away again."

"All right," I said, after standing there a moment. "But it won't do any good; it's no use."

She went away, and the fireflies, on their electric circuits, fluttered after her like an errant constellation, showing her how to walk in darkness. I heard her say, faintly, "We've got to try, anyway."

Other fireflies followed me to my room. When the weight of my body cut a circuit in the bed, the fireflies winked out. It was midnight, and my mother and I waited, our rooms separated by darkness, in bed. The bed began to rock me and sing to me. I touched a switch; the singing and rocking stopped. I didn't want to sleep. I didn't want to sleep at all.

This night was no different from a thousand others in our time. We would wake nights and feel the cool air turn hot, feel the fire in the wind, or see the walls burned a bright color for an instant, and then we knew *his* rocket was over our house—his rocket, and the oak trees swaying from the concussion. And I would lie there, eyes wide, panting, and mother in her room. Her voice would come to me over the interroom radio:

"Did you feel it?"

And I would answer, "That was him, all right."

That was my father's ship passing over our town, a small town where *space* rockets never came, and we would lie awake for the next two hours, thinking, "Now Dad's landed in Springfield, now he's on the tarmac, now he's signing the papers, now he's in the helicopter, now he's over the river, now the hills, now he's settling the helicopter in at the little airport at Green Village here. . . ." And the night would be half over when, in our separate cool beds, Mother and I would be listening, listening. "Now he's walking down Bell Street. He always walks . . . never takes a cab . . . now across the park, now turning the corner of Oakhurst and *now* . . ."

I lifted my head from my pillow. Far down the street, coming closer and closer, smartly, quickly, briskly—footsteps. Now turning in at our house, up the porch steps. And we were both smiling in the cool darkness, Mom and I, when we heard the front door open in recognition, speak a quiet word of welcome, and shut, downstairs. . . .

Three hours later I turned the brass knob to their room quietly, holding my breath, balancing in a darkness as big as the space between the planets, my hand out to reach the small black case at the foot of my parents' sleeping bed. Taking it, I ran silently to my room, thinking, he won't tell me, he doesn't want me to *know*.

And from the opened case spilled his black uniform, like a black nebula, stars glittering here or there, distantly, in the material. I kneaded the dark stuff in my warm hands; I smelled the planet Mars, an iron smell, and the planet Venus, a green ivy smell, and the planet Mercury, a scent of sulphur and fire; and I could smell the milky moon and the hardness of stars. I pushed the uniform into a centrifuge machine I'd built in my ninth-grade shop that year, set it whirling. Soon a fine powder precipitated into a retort. This I slid under a microscope. And while my parents slept unaware, and while our house was asleep, all the automatic bakers and servers and robot cleaners in an electric slumber, I stared down upon brilliant motes of meteor dust, comet tail, and loam from far Jupiter glistening like worlds themselves which drew me down the tube a billion miles into space, at terrific accelerations.

At dawn, exhausted with my journey and fearful of discovery, I returned the boxed uniform to their sleeping room.

Then I slept, only to waken at the sound of the horn of the dry-cleaning car which stopped in the yard below. They took the black uniform box with them. It's good I didn't wait, I thought. For the uniform would be back in an hour, clean of all its destiny and travel.

I slept again, with the little vial of magical dust in my pajama pocket, over my beating heart.

When I came downstairs, there was Dad at the breakfast table, biting into his toast. "Sleep good, Doug?" he said, as if he had been here all the time, and hadn't been gone for three months.

"All right," I said.

"Toast?"

He pressed a button and the breakfast table made me four pieces, golden brown.

I remember my father that afternoon, digging and digging in the garden, like an animal after something, it seemed. There he was with his long dark arms moving swiftly, planting, tamping, fixing, cutting, pruning, his dark face always down to the soil, his eyes always down to what he was doing, never up to the sky, never looking at me, or Mother, even, unless we knelt with him to feel the earth soak up through the overalls at our knees, to put our hands into the black

256 dirt and not look at the bright, crazy sky. Then he would glance to either side, to Mother or me, and give us a gentle wink, and go on, bent down, face down, the sky staring at his back.

That night we sat on the mechanical porch swing which swung us and blew a wind upon us and sang to us. It was summer and moonlight and we had lemonade to drink, and we held the cold glasses in our hands, and Dad read the stereo-newspapers inserted into the special hat you put on your head and which turned the microscopic page in front of the magnifying lens if you blinked three times in succession. Dad smoked cigarettes and told me about how it was when he was a boy in the year 1997. After a while he said, as he had always said, "Why aren't you out playing kick-the-can, Doug?"

I didn't say anything, but Mom said, "He does, on nights when you're not here."

Dad looked at me and then, for the first time that day, at the sky. Mother always watched him when he glanced at the stars. The first day and night when he got home he wouldn't look at the sky much. I thought about him gardening and gardening so furiously, his face almost driven into the earth. But the second night he looked at the stars a little more. Mother wasn't afraid of the sky in the day so much, but it was the night stars that she wanted to turn off, and sometimes I could almost see her reaching for a switch in her mind, but never finding it. And by the third night maybe Dad'd be out here on the porch until 'way after we were all ready for bed, and then I'd hear Mom call him in, almost like she called me from the street at times. And then I would hear Dad fitting the electric-eye door lock in place, with a sigh. And the next morning at breakfast I'd glance down and see his little black case near his feet as he buttered his toast and Mother slept late.

"Well, be seeing you, Doug," he'd say, and we'd shake hands.

"In about three months?"

"Right."

And he'd walk away down the street, not taking a helicopter or beetle or bus, just walking with his uniform hidden in his small underarm case; he didn't want anyone to think he was vain about being a Rocket Man.

Mother would come out to eat breakfast, one piece of dry toast, about an hour later.

But now it was tonight, the first night, the good night, and he wasn't looking at the stars much at all.

"Let's go to the television carnival," I said.

"Fine," said Dad.

Mother smiled at me.

And we rushed off to town in a helicopter and took Dad through a thousand exhibits, to keep his face and head down with us and not looking anywhere else. And as we laughed at the funny things and looked serious at the serious ones, I thought, My father goes to Saturn and Neptune and Pluto, but he never brings me presents. Other boys whose fathers go into space bring back bits of ore from Callisto and hunks of black meteor or blue sand. But I have to get my own collection, trading from other boys, the Martian rocks and Mercurian sands which filled my room, but about which Dad would never comment.

258   On occasion, I remembered, he brought something for
Mother. He planted some Martian sunflowers once in our
yard, but after he was gone a month and the sunflowers
grew large, Mom ran out one day and cut them all down.

Without thinking, as we paused at one of the three-
dimensional exhibits, I asked Dad the question I always
asked:

"What's it like, out in space?"

Mother shot me a frightened glance. It was too late.

Dad stood there for a full half minute trying to find an
answer, then he shrugged.

"It's the best thing in a lifetime of best things." Then he
caught himself. "Oh, it's really nothing at all. Routine. You
wouldn't like it." He looked at me, apprehensively.

"But *you* always go back."

"Habit."

"Where're you going next?"

"I haven't decided yet. I'll think it over."

He always thought it over. In those days rocket pilots
were rare and he could pick and choose work when he liked.
On the third night of his homecoming you could see him
picking and choosing among the stars.

"Come on," said Mother, "let's go home."

It was still early when we got home. I wanted Dad to put
on his uniform. I shouldn't have asked—it always made
Mother unhappy—but I could not help myself. I kept at him,
though he had always refused. I had never seen him in it,
and at last he said, "Oh, all right."

We waited in the parlor while he went upstairs in the
air flue. Mother looked at me dully, as if she couldn't believe
that her own son could do this to her. I glanced away. "I'm
sorry," I said.

"You're not helping at all," she said. "At all."

There was a whisper in the air flue a moment later.

"Here I am," said Dad quietly.

We looked at him in his uniform.

It was glossy black with silver buttons and silver rims to the heels of the black boots, and it looked as if someone had cut the arms and legs and body from a dark nebula, with little faint stars glowing through it. It fit as close as a glove fits to a slender long hand, and it smelled like cool air and metal and space. It smelled of fire and time.

Father stood, smiling awkwardly, in the center of the room.

"Turn around," said Mother.

Her eyes were remote, looking at him.

When he was gone, she never talked of him. She never said anything about anything but the weather or the condition of my neck and the need of a washcloth for it, or the fact that she didn't sleep nights. Once she said the light was too strong at night.

"But there's no moon this week," I said.

"There's starlight," she said.

I went to the store and bought her some darker, greener shades. As I lay in bed at night, I could hear her pull them down tight to the bottom of the windows. It made a long rustling noise.

Once I tried to mow the lawn.

"No." Mom stood in the door. "Put the mower away."

So the grass went three months at a time without cutting. Dad cut it when he came home.

She wouldn't let me do anything else either, like repairing the electrical breakfast maker or the mechanical book reader. She saved everything up, as if for Christmas. And then I

260 would see Dad hammering or tinkering, and always smiling at his work, and Mother smiling over him, happy.

No, she never talked of him when he was gone. And as for Dad, he never did anything to make a contact across the millions of miles. He said once, "If I called you, I'd want to be with you. I wouldn't be happy."

Once Dad said to me, "Your mother treats me, sometimes, as if I weren't here—as if I were invisible."

I had seen her do it. She would look just beyond him, over his shoulders, at his chin or hands, but never into his eyes. If she did look at his eyes, her eyes were covered with a film, like an animal going to sleep. She said yes at the right times, and smiled, but always a half second later than expected.

"I'm not there for her," said Dad.

But other days she would be there and he would be there for her, and they would hold hands and walk around the block, or take rides, with Mom's hair flying like a girl's behind her, and she would cut off all the mechanical devices in the kitchen and bake him incredible cakes and pies and cookies, looking deep into his face, her smile a real smile. But at the end of such days when he was there to her, she would always cry. And Dad would stand helpless, gazing about the room as if to find the answer, but never finding it.

Dad turned slowly, in his uniform, for us to see.

"Turn around again," said Mom.

The next morning Dad came rushing into the house with handfuls of tickets. Pink rocket tickets for California, blue tickets for Mexico.

"Come on!" he said. "We'll buy disposable clothes and
burn them when they're soiled. Look, we take the noon
rocket to L.A., the two-o'clock helicopter to Santa Barbara,
the nine-o'clock plane to Ensenada, sleep overnight!"

And we went to California and up and down the Pacific
Coast for a day and a half, settling at last on the sands of
Malibu to cook wieners at night. Dad was always listening
or singing or watching things on all sides of him, holding
onto things as if the world were a centrifuge going so swiftly
that he might be flung off away from us at any instant.

The last afternoon at Malibu Mom was up in the hotel
room. Dad lay on the sand beside me for a long time in the
hot sun. "Ah," he sighed, "this is it." His eyes were gently
closed; he lay on his back, drinking the sun. "You *miss* this,"
he said.

He meant "on the rocket," of course. But he never said
"the rocket" or mentioned the rocket and all the things you
couldn't have on the rocket. You couldn't have a salt wind on
the rocket or a blue sky or a yellow sun or Mom's cooking.
You couldn't talk to your fourteen-year-old boy on a rocket.

"Let's hear it," he said at last.

And I knew that now we would talk, as we had always
talked, for three hours straight. All afternoon we would
murmur back and forth in the lazy sun about my school
grades, how high I could jump, how fast I could swim.

Dad nodded each time I spoke and smiled and slapped
my chest lightly in approval. We talked. We did not talk of
rockets or space, but we talked of Mexico, where we had
driven once in an ancient car, and of the butterflies we had
caught in the rain forests of green warm Mexico at noon,
seeing the hundred butterflies sucked to our radiator, dying

there, beating their blue and crimson wings, twitching, beautiful, and sad. We talked of such things instead of the things I wanted to talk about. And he listened to me. That was the thing he did, as if he was trying to fill himself up with all the sounds he could hear. He listened to the wind and the falling ocean and my voice, always with a rapt attention, a concentration that almost excluded physical bodies themselves and kept only the sounds. He shut his eyes to listen. I would see him listening to the lawn mower as he cut the grass by hand instead of using the remote-control device, and I would see him smelling the cut grass as it sprayed up at him behind the mower in a green fount.

"Doug," he said, about five in the afternoon, as we were picking up our towels and heading back along the beach near the surf, "I want you to promise me something."

"What?"

"Don't ever be a Rocket Man."

I stopped.

"I mean it," he said. "Because when you're out there you want to be here, and when you're here you want to be out there. Don't start that. Don't let it get hold of you."

"But——"

"You don't know what it is. Every time I'm out there I think, If I ever get back to Earth I'll stay there; I'll never go out again. But I go out, and I guess I'll always go out."

"I've thought about being a Rocket Man for a long time," I said.

He didn't hear me. "I *try* to stay here. Last Saturday when I got home I started trying so damned hard to *stay* here."

I remembered him in the garden, sweating, and all the traveling and doing and listening, and I knew that he did this to convince himself that the sea and the towns and the land and his family were the only real things and the good things. But I knew where he would be tonight: looking at the jewelry in Orion from our front porch.

"Promise me you won't be like me," he said.

I hesitated awhile. "Okay," I said.

He shook my hand. "Good boy," he said.

The dinner was fine that night. Mom had run about the kitchen with handfuls of cinnamon and dough and pots and pans tinkling, and now a great turkey fumed on the table, with dressing, cranberry sauce, peas, and pumpkin pie.

"In the middle of August?" said Dad, amazed.

"You won't be here for Thanksgiving."

"So I won't."

He sniffed it. He lifted each lid from each tureen and let the flavor steam over his sunburned face. He said "Ah" to each. He looked at the room and his hands. He gazed at the pictures on the wall, the chairs, the table, me, and Mom. He cleared his throat. I saw him make up his mind. "Lilly?"

"Yes?" Mom looked across her table which she had set like a wonderful silver trap, a miraculous gravy pit into which, like a struggling beast of the past caught in a tar pool, her husband might at last be caught and held, gazing out through a jail of wishbones, safe forever. Her eyes sparkled.

"Lilly," said Dad.

Go on, I thought crazily. Say it, quick; say you'll stay home this time, for good, and never go away; *say* it!

Just then a passing helicopter jarred the room and the windowpane shook with a crystal sound. Dad glanced at the window.

The blue stars of evening were there, and the red planet Mars was rising in the East.

Dad looked at Mars a full minute. Then he put his hand out blindly toward me. "May I have some peas," he said.

"Excuse me," said Mother. "I'm going to get some bread." She rushed out into the kitchen.

"But there's bread on the table," I said.

Dad didn't look at me as he began his meal.

I couldn't sleep that night. I came downstairs at one in the morning and the moonlight was like ice on all the house-tops, and dew glittered in a snow field on our grass. I stood in the doorway in my pajamas, feeling the warm night wind, and then I knew that Dad was sitting in the mechanical porch swing, gliding gently. I could see his profile tilted back, and he was watching the stars wheel over the sky. His eyes were like gray crystal there, the moon in each one.

I went out and sat beside him.

We glided awhile in the swing.

At last I said, "How many ways are there to die in space?"

"A million."

"Name some."

"The meteors hit you. The air goes out of your rocket. Or comets take you along with them. Concussion. Strangula-tion. Explosion. Centrifugal force. Too much acceleration. Too little. The heat, the cold, the sun, the moon, the stars, the planets, the asteroids, the planetoids, radiation . . . "

And do they bury you?"

"They never find you."

"Where do you go?"

"A billion miles away. Traveling graves, they call them. You become a meteor or a planetoid traveling forever through space."

I said nothing.

"One thing," he said later, "it's quick in space. Death. It's over like that. You don't linger. Most of the time you don't even know it. You're dead and that's it."

We went up to bed.

It was morning.

Standing in the doorway, Dad listened to the yellow canary singing in its golden cage.

"Well, I've decided," he said. "Next time I come home, I'm home to stay."

"Dad!" I said.

"Tell your mother that when she gets up," he said.

"You *mean* it!"

He nodded gravely. "See you in about three months."

And there he went off down the street, carrying his uniform in its secret box, whistling and looking at the tall green trees and picking chinaberries off the chinaberry bush as he brushed by, tossing them ahead of him as he walked away into the bright shade of earning morning. . . .

I asked Mother about a few things that morning after Father had been gone a number of hours. "Dad said that sometimes you don't act as if you hear or see him," I said.

And then she explained everything to me quietly.

"When he went off into space ten years ago, I said to myself, 'He's dead.' Or as good as dead. So I think of him dead. And when he comes back, three or four times a year, it's not him at all, it's only a pleasant little memory or a dream. And if a memory stops or a dream stops, it can't hurt half as much. So most of the time I think of him dead——"

"But other times——"

"Other times I can't help myself. I bake pies and treat him as if he were alive, and then it hurts. No, it's better to think he hasn't been here for ten years and I'll never see him again. It doesn't hurt as much."

"Didn't he say next time he'd settle down."

She shook her head slowly. "No, he's dead. I'm very sure of that."

"He'll come alive again, then," I said.

"Ten years ago," said Mother, "I thought, What if he dies on Venus? Then we'll never be able to see Venus again. What if he dies on Mars? We'll never be able to look at Mars again, all red in the sky, without wanting to go in and lock the door. Or what if he died on Jupiter or Saturn or Neptune? On those nights when those planets were high in the sky, we wouldn't want to have anything to do with the stars."

"I guess not," I said.

The message came the next day.

The messenger gave it to me and I read it standing on the porch. The sun was setting. Mom stood in the screen door behind me, watching me fold the message and put it in my pocket.

"Mom," I said.

"Don't tell me anything I don't already know," she said.

She didn't cry.

Well, it wasn't Mars, and it wasn't Venus, and it wasn't Jupiter or Saturn that killed him. We wouldn't have to think of him every time Jupiter or Saturn or Mars lit up the evening sky.

This was different.

His ship had fallen into the sun.

And the sun was big and fiery and merciless, and it was always in the sky and you couldn't get away from it.

So for a long time after my father died my mother slept through the days and wouldn't go out. We had breakfast at midnight and lunch at three in the morning, and dinner at the cold dim hour of 6 A.M. We went to all-night shows and went to bed at sunrise.

And, for a long while, the only days we ever went out to walk were the days when it was raining and there was no sun.

268 About the Author

Ray Bradbury, born in 1920, began his writing career in high school, where he founded a science fiction magazine. He never went to college, working instead as a newsboy while he wrote and tried to publish his science fiction short stories. He reports that he was much influenced by the "Buck Rogers" and "Flash Gordon" comic strips of science fantasy.

Ultimately, he became a very successful writer, winning national awards and recognition, something unusual for writers of science fiction. Several of his stories have appeared in collections of *The Best Short Stories of the Year*. Some of his works have been made into moving pictures, notably *Fahrenheit 451* (1966) and *The Illustrated Man* (1969). Other stories have been adapted for television presentations.

Despite his interest in inventions of the future and space travel, Ray Bradbury has never driven a car nor flown in an airplane. He gets around mostly on his bicycle.

FOR DISCUSSION

1. One of the attractions of science fiction stories is the picture they offer of possible life in the future.

   a. Scattered throughout this story are references to inventions that make future life on Earth easier and quite different from what it is today. Try to list as many of these inventions as you can find, beginning with the "electric fireflies" in the first paragraph. Explain what the actual usefulness of each invention might be.

b. On the whole, do you feel you would prefer to live **269** in a world of such inventions, or do you prefer living as we do today. Explain your reasons.

2. Each of the characters in this story—the boy, his mother, his father—exhibits strange behavior on certain occasions.

    a. What is strange about the boy's behavior on the night of his father's arrival? How do you explain his behavior?

    b. Cite several instances of strange behavior on the part of the boy's mother, and explain why she might have acted as she did in each instance.

    c. On what occasions did the father act strangely? How do you explain his behavior?

3. Among the odd things about Doug's father, did you notice that, unlike other fathers who were rocket men, he never brought presents from outer space for his son? Why do you suppose he didn't do so?

4. What does each of these quotations tell us about Doug's mother?

    a. Once she said the light was too strong at night (for sleep).
    "But there's no moon," I said.
    "There's starlight," she said. (page 259)

    b. "No, it's better to think he hasn't been here for ten years and I'll never see him again. It doesn't hurt so much."

5. What does each of these quotations tell us about Doug's father?

  a. "What's it like, out in space?"
  "It's the best thing in a life time of best things . . . Oh, it's really nothing at all. Routine. You wouldn't like it." (page 258)

  b. Dad was always listening or singing or watching things on all sides of him, holding onto things as if the world were a centrifuge going so swiftly that he might be flung off away from us at any instant. (page 261)

  c. "Promise me you won't be like me," he said. (page 263)

6. One of the best known ancient Greek myths tells of Daedalus, an ingenious inventor who devised wings for flying, both for himself and his son, Icarus. Daedalus warned his son not to fly too high, but Icarus, being young and rash, flew up close to the sun, whereupon his wings (made of wax) were melted, and he died.

  a. What truth about the ambitions of Man and the possible results of such ambitions may be symbolized (represented) in this ancient myth?

  b. What possible connections may there be between the story of the Rocket Man and the myth of Daedalus and Icarus? Note particularly the concluding part of the story.

7. Do you think young Douglas might have grown up to be a Rocket Man? Support your answer.

VOCABULARY GROWTH

A knowledge of the meaning of certain scientific words commonly used in connection with outer space may help considerably in our understanding of this story. In your dictionary, look up the meaning of each *italicized* word in the following quotations from the story, and then explain the meaning of the word.

1. She went away, and the fireflies, on their electric circuits, fluttered after her like an errant (wandering) *constellation.* (page 253)

2. And from the opened case spilled his black uniform, like a black *nebula,* stars glittering here or there, distantly, in the material. (page 254)

3. I pushed the uniform into a *centrifuge* machine I'd built . . . Soon a white powder *precipitated* into a retort (a closed laboratory bottle). (page 254)

4. At last I said, "How many ways are there to die in space?" . . . "The *meteors* hit you . . . or *comets* take you along with them. . . . *Centrifugal* force. Too much *acceleration.* . . . The heat, the cold, the moon, the stars, the planets, the *asteroids,* the *planetoids, radiation* . . ." (page 264)

FOR COMPOSITION

1. In the light of this story, and in the light of other ideas you may have, do you think we ought to push ahead vigorously with our explorations of space. Or should we call a halt? Write a composition in which you consider this question and explain the reasons for your opinions.

272   **2.** Write a composition in which you explain how you
       would feel and what you would do if someone in your
       family volunteered to become an astronaut and to
       receive training to visit other planets.

       3. From all you know of the moon and the planets do you
       think that you would like to visit them, or even live
       there if it ever became possible? Explain your point of
       view and reasons in a composition.

The Fun They Had

ISAAC ASIMOV

Have you ever found school boring? Does the idea
of education by TV at home appeal to you?
Imagine yourself living in the year 2157. Yes! You
have it—school in your own home on a TV screen!

MARGIE EVEN wrote about it that night in her diary.
On the page headed May 17, 2157, she wrote, "Today Tommy
found a real book!"

It was a very old book. Margie's grandfather once said
that when he was a little boy *his* grandfather told him that
there was a time when all stories were printed on paper.

They turned the pages, which were yellow and crinkly,
and it was awfully funny to read words that stood still instead of moving the way they were supposed to—on a screen,
you know. And then, when they turned back to the page

274 before, it had the same words on it that it had had when they read it the first time.

"Gee," said Tommy, "what a waste. When you're through with the book, you just throw it away, I guess. Our television screen must have had a million books on it and it's good for plenty more. I wouldn't throw *it* away."

"Same with mine," said Margie. She was eleven and hadn't seen as many telebooks as Tommy had. He was thirteen.

She said, "Where did you find it?"

"In my house," He pointed without looking, because he was busy reading. "In the attic."

"What's it about?"

"School."

Margie was scornful. "School? What's there to write about school? I hate school."

Margie always hated school, but now she hated it more than ever. The mechanical teacher had been giving her test after test in geography and she had been doing worse and worse until her mother had shaken her head sorrowfully and sent for the County Inspector.

He was a round little man with a red face and a whole box of tools with dials and wires. He smiled at Margie and gave her an apple, then took the teacher apart. Margie had hoped he wouldn't know how to put it together again, but he knew how all right, and, after an hour or so, there it was again, large and black and ugly, with a big screen on which all the lessons were shown and the questions were asked. That wasn't so bad. The part Margie hated most was the slot where she had to put homework and test papers. She always had to write them out in a punch code they made her learn when she was six years old, and the mechanical teacher calculated the mark in no time.

The Inspector had smiled after he was finished and patted Margie's head. He said to her mother, "It's not the little girl's fault, Mrs. Jones. I think the geography sector was geared a little too quick. Those things happen sometimes. I've slowed it up to an average ten-year level. Actually, the over-all pattern of her progress is quite satisfactory." And he patted Margie's head again.

Margie was disappointed. She had been hoping they would take the teacher away altogether. They had once taken Tommy's teacher away for nearly a month because the history sector had blanked out completely.

So she said to Tommy, "Why would anyone write about school?"

Tommy looked at her with very superior eyes. "Because it's not our kind of school, stupid. This is the old kind of school that they had hundreds and hundreds of years ago." He added loftily, pronouncing the word carefully, *"Centuries ago."*

Margie was hurt. "Well, I don't know what kind of school they had all that time ago." She read the book over his shoulder for a while, then said, "Anyway, they had a teacher."

"Sure they had a teacher, but it wasn't a *regular* teacher. It was a man."

"A man? How could a man be a teacher?"

"Well, he just told the boys and girls things and gave them homework and asked them questions."

"A man isn't smart enough."

"Sure he is. My father knows as much as my teacher."

"He can't. A man can't know as much as a teacher."

"He knows almost as much, I betcha."

Margie wasn't prepared to dispute that. She said, "I wouldn't want a strange man in my house to teach me."

Tommy screamed with laughter. "You don't know much,

276   Margie. The teachers didn't live in the house. They had a special building and all the kids went there."

"And all the kids learned the same thing?"

"Sure, if they were the same age."

"But my mother says a teacher has to be adjusted to fit the mind of each boy and girl it teaches and that each kid has to be taught differently."

"Just the same they didn't do it that way then. If you don't like it, you don't have to read the book."

"I didn't say I didn't like it," Margie said quickly. She wanted to read about those funny schools.

They weren't even half-finished when Margie's mother called, "Margie! School!"

Margie looked up. "Not yet, Mamma."

"Now!" said Mrs. Jones. "And it's probably time for Tommy, too."

Margie said to Tommy, "Can I read the book some more with you after school?"

"Maybe," he said nonchalantly. He walked away whistling, the dusty old book tucked beneath his arm.

Margie went into the schoolroom. It was right next to her bedroom, and the mechanical teacher was on and waiting for her. It was always on at the same time every day except Saturday and Sunday, because her mother said little girls learned better if they learned at regular hours.

The screen was lit up, and it said: "Today's arithmetic lesson is on the addition of proper fractions. Please insert yesterday's homework in the proper slot."

Margie did so with a sigh. She was thinking about the old schools they had when her grandfather's grandfather was a little boy. All the kids from the whole neighborhood came, laughing and shouting in the schoolyard, sitting together in the schoolroom, going home together at the end of

the day. They learned the same things, so they could help one 277
another on the homework and talk about it.

And the teachers were people....

The mechanical teacher was flashing on the screen: "When we add the fractions ½ and ¼——"

Margie was thinking about how the kids must have loved it in the old days. She was thinking about the fun they had.

About the Author

Isaac Asimov, born in Russia in 1920, living today in Massachusetts, is one of a small group of distinguished scientists who have turned their hands to writing science fiction. He is a professor of biochemistry at the Boston University School of Medicine, with many books to his credit in the fields of biology, mathematics, and physics. He is most popularly known, however, for his imaginative short stories and novels, in which he not only recounts fantastic events, but also makes us do some hard thinking about where the world is going.

FOR DISCUSSION

Understanding the Story

1. The story begins with the discovery in 2157 of an old book. What do the children find so strange about this book?

   What differences between life in general two hundred years from now and life today are suggested to you by the first incident in this story?

2. According to the story, what differences will there be in the schooling of children two hundred years from now?

3. The story suggests some of the advantages which this type of schooling is supposed to have. What are these advantages?

4. How would you like to get your education as Margie and Tommy got theirs?

5. Reread the last paragraph. What do you suppose must have been in Margie's mind to make her feel as she did?

Was she right or wrong?

6. Mr. Asimov, the author, is fond of using irony in his stories.

Generally, there are two types of irony in stories. In some instances, the events of a story are ironical because they are the opposite of what one would normally expect. You may remember that in "What Men Live By," the one man who seemed so rich and strong that "death couldn't touch him" died very quickly thereafter. This is called the "irony of fate."

In other instances, the author wants the reader to realize that although a character means one thing in his thoughts or by his remarks, the truth is really quite different from or even the opposite of what the character thinks it is.

Mr. Asimov is especially fond of using this latter form of irony. Here are some passages from "The Fun They Had" which show his skill in using it. See if you can explain the irony in each passage:

a. "They turned the pages, which were yellow and crinkly, and it was awfully funny to read words that stood still instead of moving the way they were supposed to—on a screen, you know. And when they turned back to the page before, it had the same words on it that it had had when they read it the first time.

" 'Gee,' said Tommy, " 'what a waste ' "

b. " '. . . Anyway, they had a teacher.'
" 'Sure they had a teacher, but it wasn't a *regular* teacher. It was a man.' "

c. "Margie was thinking about how the kids must have loved it in the old days. She was thinking about the fun they had."

VOCABULARY GROWTH

Using Word Parts to Unlock Word Meanings

You will recall the value of knowing the meanings of certain prefixes or other word parts which appear in our language. They enable you to guess intelligently at the meanings of new words which contain them.

1. a. In "The Fun They Had" *television* is important. *Tele* in Greek meant "far off." Can you see why the name *television* was given to this invention?

b. On page 276 the author mentions the word *telebook.* Actually there is no such word today, but the author wants you to imagine that in 2157 there will be such a word and such a thing. What do you imagine a *telebook* would be?

c. List five other words beginning with *tele* Explain why each word begins with this prefix.

2. On page 276 we learn that Margie has trouble with *geography.* This word comes from two Greek words— *geo,* meaning "earth" or "ground," and *graphein,* meaning "write" or "draw."

a. Here are some other words beginning with geo. Find their meanings and see what connection they have with "earth" or "ground."
geology   geometry   geochemistry

b. Here are some words that contain *graph.* Look them up and see what each has to do with "writing" or "drawing."
telegraph   autograph   stenography   seismograph

FOR COMPOSITION

1. Margie would have liked to go to school in the 1900's.
Most of us realize that our schools are not perfect. What,
to you, is the most important fault in our schools?
Write a composition in which you explain this fault and
suggest a remedy.

2. You can probably prophesy a different kind of schooling
in the future. Write a composition describing your own
picture of schooling a hundred years from now.

3. Consider the pictures of everyday life in the future presented in "The Rocket Man" and in this story, particularly the new inventions that might influence our everyday activities. Write a composition in which you explain
why you would or would not enjoy living in such a
society. Do you see any sharp difference between the
life of the future as presented by Bradbury and by
Asimov?

ACKNOWLEDGMENTS

(continued from page iv)

Harold Ober Associates Inc.: For "Thicker Than Water," by Paul Gallico. Copyright 1944 by The Crowell-Collier Publishing Co.

Oxford University Press: For "What Men Live By," from *Twenty-Three Tales*, by Leo Tolstoy, translated by L. and A. Maude.

Pan American Union: For "Lather and Nothing Else," by Heranado Téllez. Reprinted from *Americas*, monthly magazine published by the Pan American Union in English, Spanish, and Portuguese.

Laurence Pollinger Limited: For "The Summer of the Beautiful White Horse," from *My Name Is Aram*, by William Saroyan. Published by Faber and Faber Limited.

Charles Scribner's Sons: For "Midnight," reprinted with the permission of Charles Scribner's Sons from *Sun Up* by Will James. Copyright 1931 Charles Scribner's Sons; renewal copyright © 1959 Auguste Default. "Death of a Tsotsi" is reprinted with the permission of Charles Scribner's Sons from *Tales From a Troubled Land* by Alan Paton. Copyright © 1961 Alan Paton.

Harold Matson Company, Inc.: For "The Rocket Man" by Ray Bradbury. Copyright 1951 by Ray Bradbury. Reprinted by permission of Harold Matson Co., Inc.